How

WAL★MART

Is Destroying

America

(and the World)

How

WAL★MART

Is Destroying

America

(and the World)

And What You Can Do About It

Bill Quinn

TEN SPEED PRESS
Berkeley | Toronto

THIRD EDITION

Copyright © 2005, 2000, 1998 by Bill Quinn.

Ten Speed Press
Box 7123
Berkeley, California 94707
www.tenspeed.com

Distributed in Australia by Simon & Schuster Australia, in
Canada by Ten Speed Press Canada, in New Zealand by
Southern Publishers Group, in South Africa by Real Books,
and in the United Kingdom and Europe by Airlift Book
Company.

Writing assistance by Kristi Hein
Text design by Toni Tajima
Cover design by Lisa Patrizio
Illustrations by Ivar Diehl

Library of Congress Cataloging-in-Publication Data
Quinn, Bill, 1912 May 15–
    How Wal-Mart is destroying America (and the world) and
what you can do about it / Bill Quinn.—3rd ed.
        p. cm.
    ISBN-10: 1-58008-668-3
    ISBN-13: 978-1-58008-668-4
    1. Wal-Mart (firm)   2. Discount house (Retail trade)—
United States.   3. Retail Trade—United States—Personnel
management.   4. Small business—United States.   I. Title.
HF5429.2.Q56 2005
381'149'0973—dc22

                                                2005008980

Printed in the United States
First printing this edition, 2005

2 3 4 5 6 7 8 9 10 — 09 08 07 06 05

DEDICATION

To Lennie Quinn, my wife of fifty-nine years, without whom I couldn't find my way to the bathroom.

To my son Rix, who took over the family publishing business twenty-six years ago and freed up the old man to write personal stuff, like this anti–Wal-Mart book.

To Phil Wood, president of Ten Speed Press, who shares my feelings on Walton Enterprises . . . and tells you why in his "Letter from the Publisher."

To Kristi Hein, the talented wordsmith who worked with me again to bring this book up to date on the latest Wal-Mart "shenanigans."

CONTENTS

In 1998 I was happy to publish the first edition of this book. At the time, I thought I was just doing my old friend, author Bill Quinn a favor at the same time as I was taking a position on a company that had caused us more than just a headache.

In 1995, Sam's Clubs, a division of the huge Wal-Mart Corporation, bought almost 30,000 books from us, paying close to a quarter of a million dollars. Two months after we'd shipped them out, they sent back more than half of the order, requesting a refund for unsold merchandise. Worse yet, almost 70 percent of the returned books were so badly damaged that they couldn't be re-sold. Wal-Mart lacked a central warehouse so merchandise was sent back from individual stores, using whatever they had for packing material—in a couple of cases that meant baling wire!

That first edition struck a chord in readers all across America, more so than we ever imagined or dreamed. It sold more than 20,000 copies. It also generated loads of calls and letters, helping Bill and his supporters establish and sustain a network of hundreds of people all over this country, often with legitimate axes to grind against the Walton family empire.

In 2000 we published the second edition, which bore a new title to alert readers to a wider threat: Wal-Mart had spread way beyond the borders of the United States and was profoundly challenging businesses and communities worldwide by setting a new standard that suppliers and communities are forced to follow.

This third edition brings us current with the recent legal

debates about healthcare costs, female worker compensation, and anti-union activities.

If Wal-Mart stores are inappropriate for your community you should read this book . . . and if you think they're okay, well, you should also read this book to find out what's coming!

My friends and fellow anti-Wal-martians,

As I write this preface to the third edition near the end of my deadline, there's bad news and good news on the Wal-Mart front.

First, the bad news. Since our second edition in 2000, Wal-Mart has just kept on getting bigger and badder:

More stores. Wal-Mart has added over 1,100 stores worldwide, and that increase is *net*—it includes all the stores closed for consolidation and old discount stores that were converted to more colossal Supercenters. That's a 27 percent increase, with the global store count well past 1,500.

More sales. Wal-Mart's worldwide net sales in 2004 were $276 billion. Our second edition reported sales of $165 billion; our first edition, $100 billion.

More "associates." One and a half million folks around the world toil for Wal-Mart, most of them wearing the blue vest of the in-store "associate." There's a sad truth behind the sunny smiles of the workers in Wal-Mart's commercials: part-time hours or unpaid overtime, poverty-level wages, unafford-able benefits, and forced cheerleading for "The Company." And because Bentonville is now the world's largest private em-ployer, its treatment of its employees forces competing retail-ers to be equally stingy and heartless in order to survive.

More market dominance. In 2002, 82 percent of U.S. households bought something at Wal-Mart. Wal-Mart sells about 30 percent of all U.S. household consumables (sham-poo, toilet paper, and the like), 15 to 20 percent of music and movie discs and tapes, 19 percent of groceries, and 16 per-cent of pharmaceuticals.

More destruction of U.S. jobs. Wal-Mart has its suppliers by the short hairs and is a major force in driving manufacturers and jobs overseas. Forget about "Buy American"; Wal-Mart brings in well over 10 percent of all imports from China, and that's just one of the many countries where sweatshop laborers make pennies a day to produce Wal-Mart's $9.99 fans and $7.36 T-shirts.

More obscene wealth for the Walton family. Depending on the current price of Wal-Mart stock, these five share a fortune in shares and liquid assets of some $102 billion. (Just 1 percent of that could provide the decent health-care coverage that every "associate" on the payroll *doesn't* have now.)

Now for the *good news*: The world has woken up and is fighting back. We may not have Wal-Mart on the run—not yet—but the Bentonvillains are on the defensive. Just look at some of the high-profile coverage they've been getting: In the last few years, Wal-Mart's been scrutinized by major metropolitan dailies like the *New York Times* ("States Are Battling Against Wal-Mart Over Health Care"), the *Wall Street Journal* ("Wal-Mart Cost-Cutting Finds a Big Target in Health Benefits"), and the *Los Angeles Times* (with a three-part series, "An Empire Built on Bargains Remakes the Working World") and periodicals like *Business Week* (cover story "Is Wal-Mart Too Powerful?"), *Fast Company* ("The Wal-Mart You Don't Know"), and *Fortune* ("Wal-Mart Keeps the Change); in November 2004, *Fortune* offered a peek "Inside America's Richest Family," an unprecedented thirteen-page profile of the Walton family.

In a single week in November 2004, two documentaries tackled Wal-Mart. "The Age of Wal-Mart: Inside America's Most Powerful Company" was aired on CNBC, and the PBS series *Frontline* showed "Is Wal-Mart Good for America?" a look at Wal-Mart's early grasp of the information technology that powered its rise in the United States, its China connection, and its crushing effect on American business, society, and livelihoods.

When last we published, Wal-Mart had the easy upper hand in court. They hated to settle and rarely did. Their lawyers fought tough and easily outspent their poorly funded opponents.

These days, Wal-Mart faces serious and well-publicized legal challenges. Class-action suits—representing thousands of plaintiffs with a common grievance—are under way for gender and racial discrimination, unpaid overtime, unfair treatment of illegal workers, and more.

Yes, Wal-Mart's finally squirming under the microscope of legal scrutiny, media criticism, and public disapproval. So Wal-Mart has gone into major damage-control mode. In September 2004, CEO Lee Scott told an analysts' conference, "We have got to eliminate this constant barrage of negatives that cause people . . . to wonder if Wal-Mart will be allowed to grow. Our message has not gotten out to the extent that it should." Or maybe, just maybe, it finally has.

Bentonville on the defensive ain't a pretty sight, but we much prefer it to the smug, cocky Bentonville of a few years back.

For new readers, here's a little background on the author to put this anti–Wal-Mart crusade in perspective:

My dad was a small-town railroad agent who prided himself on knowing virtually everyone in the towns—three in Louisiana and four in Texas—where he worked. Pa Quinn finally settled in Grand Saline, down in beautiful East Texas, in 1920. (See map on page 21.)

He sank deep roots there, becoming a deacon in the Baptist church and an elected member of the school board. At the age of forty-six, he and my mother built their very first—and only—home.

I inherited Pa's small-townitis and, at age fifteen, I announced to an unlistening world that I was going to grow up to be a newspaper editor. I cut my eyeteeth in publishing in three small Texas towns: first in Van, population about one thousand; then Grand Saline, with about two thousand people; then Mineola, with some four thousand.

In World War II, I served thirty-two months overseas; first with the Third Infantry Division, then at VI Corps Headquarters, where I was editor of a daily mobile newspaper started in Anzio, Italy—called, fittingly, the *Beachhead News*.

When I was discharged, I moved to Fort Worth and got into the trade journal publishing business. I continued to run our magazines in a highly personalized, country-newspaper style, making a better-than-average living until I finally retired—at age eighty-four.

But deep down inside, I never left "home"—Grand Saline, Texas. When someone asks me where I live, I still nod my head toward East Texas.

How's Grand Saline doing these days? There isn't a Wal-Mart there. Yet, only thirteen miles to the east in Mineola and thirteen miles to the south in Canton, Wal-Mart has Supercenters that have claimed well over half of Grand Saline's retail business.

Grand Saline once had three thriving independent dry goods stores. Now there's none.

The first casualty was a department store owned and operated by my wife's uncle for almost seventy years. The second was a department store that had to close its doors after being in business for over fifty years. The third locked its doors for good on New Year's Day, 1998. Other independent stores in the town have suffered proportionately.

It's been estimated that for each Wal-Mart store in existence, one hundred family-owned businesses have gone under. Which adds up to—what?—half a million mom-and-pop store owners tearfully telling their children that there will be no money if misfortune comes their way.

What really stirred me to first assemble stories for this book was a 1991 story in *Fortune* magazine. A *Fortune* reporter followed the late Sam Walton around for a week. His impression of the Arkansas genius:

> And finally, there is the ruthless, predatory Sam, who stalks competitors—in any size, shape, or form—and finds sport in blasting them from the sky like so many quail.

Sam Walton's business principles laid the foundation for the ruthless corporation that has become the most feared retailer in world history:

✪ A company that got its start by building cheap, ugly, giant-size stores on the outskirts of small towns, and discounting prices so much that virtually every store in a once-proud downtown district had to close.

✪ A company that promised lots of new jobs to a small town—not bothering to tell the city fathers that most would pay near-poverty wages and some 40 percent of the "associates" would work less than the customary forty hours.

✪ A company that, to gain the support of small-town newspapers, started off as a good advertiser . . . then, once established, dropped virtually all newspaper advertising.

✪ A company that, to gain entrance to a new area, promised to become "part and parcel" of small-town America . . . and is now its worst citizen.

We're not alone in our crusade, of course. Anti–Wal-Mart campaigns have sprung up across the country. But fighting Wal-Mart is harder than David fighting Goliath. One way or the other, the Arkansas discounter generally squeezes its way in—often pressuring courts to decide in its favor.

As of 2004, the closely knit Walton family owned a 39-percent interest in Wal-Mart that is worth near the $90 billion mark. But Walton Enterprises is showing no interest in slowing its greed.

Wal-Mart's strong anti-union stance became known in the early Sam Walton days. Old Sam said he wouldn't be intimidated by unions, ever, under any circumstance. And today, with close to 1.2 million people working for Wal-Mart in America (and more than 330,000 in other countries), not a single U.S. store is unionized. In our second edition, we had high hopes that meat packers would get the union protection they voted for in Jacksonville, Texas, but Wal-Mart weaseled out of it.

City councils throughout the United States share a good deal of blame for the devastating effect Wal-Mart has had on almost every town and city it has invaded. The governing body of each municipality has a fair amount of power to slow or stop Wal-Mart or to refuse to change zoning to suit the retailer.

Local and state governments are just beginning to take steps to combat one of the biggest cancers that has ever grown on American business and society. At the federal level, both the White House and Congress seem more blind than ever to the threat—despite the bitter lessons of Enron, WorldCom, and other corporate scandals. But we're keeping an eye on those class-action lawsuits. If they reach the high courts, federal investigation and legislation could follow. We can dream, anyway.

What Is Wal-Mart?

It's the biggest retailer in the world, with worldwide net sales of $276 billion in 2004. In our first edition, published in 1998, the figure was just $100 billion!

It's the biggest private employer in the United States. As of March 2004, more than 1,500,000 people worked for Walton Enterprises worldwide. As of November 30, 2004, the company had 3,661 U.S. outlets (a net increase of 641 since the 2000 edition of this book): 1,363 discount stores, 1,672 Supercenters, 550 Sam's Clubs, and 76 Neighborhood Markets. Internationally, the company operated 1,517 units (554 added since the 2000 edition), in Argentina (11), Brazil (148), Canada (246), China (42), Germany (92), Mexico (687), Puerto Rico (54), South Korea (16), and United Kingdom (277). It's also busy acquiring stock in the Japanese Seiyu retail chain, with a goal of owning 69.4 percent by the end of 2007. In fiscal year 2004 (ending January 30, 2005) Wal-Mart planned to add about 250 net new stores, comprising 50 million square feet of retail space—an 8 percent increase.

Wal-Mart has already monopolized small-town America, and the bullies from Bentonville, Arkansas, have invaded small cities and bedroom communities with their Sam's Clubs, Supercenters, and Neighborhood Markets. The Supercenter invasion is intended to make Wal-Mart the number-one grocer in the nation.

A government that saw Standard Oil and AT&T as monopolies ain't seen nothing yet.

Wal-Mart doesn't want just some of America's business . . . *they want it all!*

And then there's the rest of the world. Wal-Mart now has a massive presence in what they call the "big three"— Canada, Britain, and Mexico—and dozens of stores in Argentina, Brazil, China, Germany, South Korea, and Puerto Rico. In Japan, Wal-Mart owns more than a one-third share in the Seiyu retail chain. Taking over an existing chain is often Wal-Mart's first step toward retail dominance in another country—it's now the number one retailer in Canada and Mexico as well as the United States.

Will the U.S. government stand up to them? Don't bet on it. Sam Walton always shunned politics—as recently as 1998, Bentonville spent zip on lobbying—but the company is now muscling in on Capitol Hill. A March 24, 2004 *Wall Street Journal* story said Wal-Mart had five DC lobbyists and "a bench of hired guns led by Thomas Hale Boggs Jr., one of [the] best-known lawyer-lobbyists," and its PAC (political action committee) was the second biggest in the capital, giving over $1 million to federal parties and candidates in 2003. Who gets the money? Candidates who share the company's priorities, such as "free trade" and freedom from union labor. Eighty-five percent of Wal-Mart's PAC donations went to Republican candidates (most corporations are careful to give about evenly to both parties).

If our elected representatives could ever pull their hands out of the PAC money trough, they might finally do something to rein in a company apparently without scruples; a company that's now not only the biggest retailer in the United States, but the biggest in the world; a company whose mushrooming size and power have permanently skewed not only the workings of America's "free market" system, but the global economy as well.

Until then, *it's up to all the rest of us to fight back.*

SEVEN BAD THINGS THAT HAPPEN WHEN WAL-MART COMES TO TOWN

Let's say it's your town. It's not big—maybe five thousand to thirty thousand folks live there, with all the businesses and services that would serve that many people. Probably, the town's not growing—and that worries some. Some think that a big retailer might help—something flashy to pull in people and money from a wider area.

So now, all of a sudden, there's a 155,000-square-foot "box" store out along the interstate, just barely inside the city limits—but definitely not "downtown." There's a sea of asphalt and a curtain of cyclone fencing where there used to be farmland or a trailer park or woods. Sam's in your town now, and he's ready to pull in the commerce from thirty-five miles around and more.

Here's what that will likely mean to you and your town.

BAD THING #1:
Store Owners Take the Biggest Hit

If you're a store owner, and your business is in direct competition with Wal-Mart (that is, you sell hardware, pharmaceu-

ticals, general merchandise, groceries, whatever), you already know you've got the fight of your life on your hands. Wal-Mart's sheer size gives it incredible advantages.

- ✪ Wal-Mart's arrival is no longer accompanied by the excitement and anticipation of yore. Word has spread, we're happy to note, and many communities are ready and unwilling. But some people in your town will still want to have a Wal-Mart. For one thing, Wal-Mart has lately mounted a very slick PR campaign, all warm and fuzzy, showing cheerful "associates" and overjoyed customers. For another, times have been tough for the working-class customer that Wal-Mart targets, and they're not getting any better.

- ✪ Because Wal-Mart is so darn big, it can cut almost any deal it wants with vendors and distributors (see chapter 3).

- ✪ Wal-Mart can lure your customers with claims of convenience and low prices—in chapter 4 we let you know how (un)true those claims are—offering an easy alternative to the downtown you and your fellow merchants have worked so hard to build.

- ✪ Wal-Mart can afford to spend quite a bit on advertising and promotion—and you can bet it will, *at first*. Read on to find out just how long that spending will last.

- ✪ Wal-Mart will engage in "predatory pricing" in an attempt to drive you out of business—fast!

A new Wal-Mart on the offensive against its local competition will be willing to take losses on merchandise that those competitors sell. It'll study what you sell, then offer it for less. Let's say you are Jim, and you own Jim's Hardware in your town. Local Wal-Mart managers will find out what you are selling and at what prices; then they will stock, advertise, and sell those items at prices near or below their cost. You can't possibly compete with this practice without losing money, and chances are good that eventually you will be driven out. Wal-Mart will then be able to sell its hardware merchandise at whatever price it wishes, having eliminated the competition—you!

Wal-Mart takes its business overwhelmingly from existing businesses. Townspeople often hope that a big shiny Wal-Mart will pull in commerce from outside the town, thus bringing more money in. It will—but almost never enough to justify cannibalizing most of a small town's small businesses, which is what happens. On average, over one hundred stores eventually go out of business in the area surrounding a "Wal-ed" town.

BAD THING #2: Jobs Are Lost

One of the biggest carrots Wal-Mart holds out to struggling small towns is the promise of more jobs. If a town is not growing, this sounds really attractive: a great big new store is going to need people to work there, isn't it?

According to various studies, at least three jobs are lost for every two jobs created by a Wal-Mart. One reason for this is that Wal-Mart is said to employ from sixty-five to seventy people for each $10 million in sales; other small businesses employ 106 people for each $10 million in sales. So Wal-Mart can do more business and pay less for employee salaries—and it does.

Also, a Wal-Mart or other big retailer coming to town is not really offering new jobs in the way a manufacturer would be. People sometimes lose sight of this. If a new factory opens in town, it is truly creating jobs that did not exist before; if a new store comes to town, and that store is selling merchandise that, for the most part, was already available in the town, it is just going to be rearranging the way money already gets spent in the town. What Wal-Mart offers is not job creation, but job re-allocation and, eventually, job loss.

Ask Kelly Gray of Las Vegas. In December 2002 the 36-year-old mother of five lost her $14.68-an-hour job as a grocery clerk at Raley's—as well as a pension and her family's health insurance—after Wal-Mart moved into the grocery business and Raley's closed its eighteen area stores. Gray was quoted by the *Los Angeles Times*: "It's like somebody came and broke into your home and took something huge and important away from you. I was scared. I cried. I shook."

But couldn't she just go to work at Wal-Mart? Not at $14.68 an hour. Not with a pension and good health insurance. Keep in mind that many of the jobs Wal-Mart offers are part-time and low-paying. Chances are that a vast majority of Wal-Mart's employees work fewer than forty hours a week

(the retailer defines a "full-time" worker as someone who puts in twenty-eight hours per week and above). And perhaps 60 to 70 percent of these workers (both full- and part-timers) have no health insurance. All are being paid a low retail wage, and all are subject to work shortage or layoff at the slightest downturn in store sales.

In the same *Times* article, Wal-Mart spokesperson Mona Williams kindly reminds us that "retail and service wages are what they are" without mentioning the better wages provided by other businesses. But we have to agree with her when she says, "If you are the sole provider for your family, then maybe it's not the right place for you."

We'd even suggest that Wal-Mart isn't the right place for anybody.

BAD THING #3: Other Businesses Suffer

Businesses that are not directly competitive with Wal-Mart (the ones that don't sell the same stuff) may have a kind of wary optimism about their big new commercial neighbor. Maybe, they think, Wal-Mart will share some of its wealth in town—sort of spread it around. Don't count on it.

For one thing, when Wal-Mart sucks all the customers away from a big anchor store, neighboring businesses are left high and dry, too. The *L.A. Times* reported that the closing of eighteen Raley's supermarkets had had this ripple effect. At a UPS Store in one deserted shopping center, owner Bonnie Neisius lamented that her business was "probably down 45 percent. I just don't get the foot traffic anymore." A few doors down, florist Diana Murphy sat idle. Wal-Mart sells flowers too, she observed, and "they even deliver."

NEWSPAPERS

When Wal-Mart first comes to a town, it may come to be known as a newspaper publisher's best friend. Full-page advertisements! Color inserts! The advertising money that Sam brings feels like a bonanza. But just you wait. As soon as the local drugstores and dry goods and hardware and appliance stores have closed, Wal-Mart may decide to withdraw almost its entire advertising expenditure from your pages.

This pattern was first noted by the *Wall Street Journal* in a 1993 article. And a popular newsletter once cited two small newspaper publishers who had felt burned by Wal-Mart's abandonment:

✪ In one town in Arkansas, Wal-Mart promptly cut its local advertising down to the bone once it gained its desired market share. Wal-Mart then asked the local newspaper for publicity for its sponsorship of a local event. The publisher of the local paper, who had learned a bitter lesson from his former advertiser, told Wal-Mart to go to hell: "I don't give free publicity to companies that don't help pay the light bill around here."

"We Don't Have to Explain Our Reasons"

According to the executive director of the Arkansas Press Association (APA), three members of the APA met with Paul Higham, Wal-Mart's vice president of marketing. Their mission: to persuade Wal-Mart to advertise in the daily and weekly newspapers they represent.

The APA members were big names in newspaper circles: Barry Newton, from the Oklahoma Newspaper Advertising Bureau; Julia Jackson, from a group of newspapers in the southeastern United States; and Dennis Schick, APA executive director. As Shick tells it, they arrived expecting a private meeting with Mr. Higham. Instead, they were met by four media buyers—all relatively young, and two of them brand new at Wal-Mart.

After several minutes, Mr. Higham appeared, asking why the three of them were there. It soon became apparent he was not overly glad to see them. For the next two hours, Higham delivered a "canned and rehearsed" spiel, including these pronouncements:

★ Newspaper (advertising) costs too much to buy.

★ Newspapers have poor and decreasing quality news–editorial content.

★ Newspaper profits are too high.

The APA group asked: "Why does Wal-Mart on occasion advertise in one newspaper—and not in another very similar newspaper?"

Higham's response: "We don't have to explain our reasons for doing what we do."

What, then, can a newspaper do to earn Wal-Mart's business?

"We don't need you or anyone else to speak for us. We'll do it ourselves."

"The Death of Small-Town America"

That's the title of a documentary that an Australian TV crew shot in Grand Saline, Texas, in 2001. And they invited us along after learning from this book about what—and who—is behind the sickening sight of so many empty storefronts.

We asked a half-dozen or more of the folks most familiar with the town's happenings how many of the town's former one-hundred-plus businesses were still in operation since Wal-Mart's arrival in the area in 1980. The answer: fewer than a handful.

Thanks to Wal-Mart, in 2005 small-town America barely exists.

✪ Another publisher—we believe it was in Snyder, Texas—was invited to come by and get a picture of founder Sam Walton when he came through the town. "Thanks, but no thanks," he told the Wal-Mart manager. "If we don't have a readership worth advertising to, why should you want us to run a photograph?"

Even in Sam Walton's own hometown of Bentonville, Arkansas, Wal-Mart rarely advertises in the local paper, according to a Wal-Mart director—and Sam's own son owns the paper!

BANKS

We've been told that it's part of Wal-Mart's overall business strategy to instantly transfer its daily earnings from its stores to corporate headquarters in Bentonville, Arkansas. So, while the local bank may have accounts with Wal-Mart, the retailer is just using the bank to drain cash from the town: pour the dollars in, then pipe them out of town the next day. The bank never gets to use the capital this cash might represent, and, what's worse, the town doesn't get any benefit from it either.

One rule of thumb states that every dollar spent in a small business will get spent again one or more times before it leaves the area (more if there are not a lot of tourists and other outsiders coming into and out of the area). This means that when a dollar is spent at Wal-Mart instead of at the local hardware store, it's not just the hardware store losing that dollar in revenue. Also losing might be the local hauling company that delivers to the store or the cafe where the store manager has dinner. Instead, that dollar goes directly to the Walton family's private Fort Knox in Bentonville, where it rafts up against billions of other bucks from around the world.

Seen from a larger perspective, Wal-Mart's non-relationship with local banks can stunt a town's overall growth. Small towns often rely on their banks as engines of growth: this is where capital meets investors and new businesses are formed. But if capital is hopping on the morning flight to Arkansas every day, entrepreneurs (that is, potential employers) are left empty-handed, and they'll have to just go away or give up.

TOURISM

Is your town a charmer, like historic Sturbridge, Massachusetts, or Gig Harbor, Washington?

Do people come from outside the area to revel in your town's ambience? You may really want to think two or three times about whether Wal-Mart's big old prefab one-look-fits-all box store is going to be what those free-spending tourists want to see.

In May 2004 the National Trust for Historic Preservation placed the *entire state* of Vermont at the top of its Most Endangered Places list—blaming the invasion of Wal-Mart and

Don't Bank on Wal-Mart

Banks have other reasons to fear Wal-Mart: The giant retailer's been trying for years to break into banking itself. Having their own bank in every Wal-Mart would bring them one step closer to being that "one-stop shop"—and wipe out whatever's left of the hometown American bank.

Back in 1999, Wal-Mart was primed for a sneaky entry into the savings bank business. Wal-Mart's foot in the door? The "mere" acquisition of a one-branch savings bank in Broken Arrow, Oklahoma. But a challenge was filed with the Office of Thrift Supervision by a Bronx, New York–based organization, the Inner City Press/Community on the Move & Inner City Public Interest Law Center. This filing—followed by last-minute revisions to a piece of financial modernization legislation signed by President Clinton—staved off Wal-Mart's bid to enter the banking industry.

Did Wal-Mart keep trying? Do birds fly? In 2001 Wal-Mart nearly convinced Toronto-Dominion Bank of Canada to offer limited services in about one hundred stores, but the bank decided the regulatory barriers were too high. And the banking industry has pushed back—their lobbyists are no slouches. In March 2004 a bill passed in the U.S. House of Representatives that pretty well put the kibosh on big retailers operating their own bank branches across state lines. To qualify, Wal-Mart would have to prove that at least 85 percent of its revenue would come from its bank operations.

other big-box retailers over the past decade for altering the state's small-town character, its "special magic," as the Trust's Richard Moe puts it. Since 1993 when Vermont first made the list, Wal-Mart has planted four "relatively small" stores in the state, but preservationists say the company has plans to expand two and bring in five more. The store's arrival in Rutland (pop. 18,000) was featured in the Wal-Mart annual report, with its employees calling it the "rebirth of Rutland." According to sprawl-busters.com, the store isn't raking in quite the hoped-for profits, and in May 2004 its manager told the town they want to pull out—but Bentonville denies it.

In Lake Placid, New York, local citizens did a survey to see what tourists and visitors thought about the proposed Wal-Mart in town. The results:

✪ 4 percent of respondents said they would be disappointed to see a Wal-Mart in Lake Placid (3 percent would be pleased; 3 percent had no opinion).

✪ 95 percent said a Wal-Mart would detract from the appeal of Lake Placid (2 percent said it would add to the appeal; 3 percent said it would not affect the appeal).

✪ 72 percent said a Wal-Mart would make them less likely to visit Lake Placid again (2 percent said it would make them more likely to visit; 26 percent said they had no opinion).

Clear enough?

BAD THING #4: Downtown Dies

This is the all-too-frequent result of Wal-Mart's infiltration of a town—and it's part of the plan. Wal-Mart's formula is to provide a neatly packaged and heavily promoted alternative to downtown.

It is an essential part of Wal-Mart's expansion plan to choose a site that is not within the downtown area, and Wal-Mart's developers usually buy the land at the cheapest possible price. Wal-Mart knows where it wants to be and how it wants to operate: not in proximity to other businesses, and not in partnership with other merchants.

Wary local activist groups have done studies on what would happen to their local economies if a Wal-Mart came in, and the results are chilling (though not surprising). The Save Historic East Aurora (New York) Association projected that a new Wal-Mart in their town would "strip our retailers, and especially our Main Street business district, of 68 percent of their existing sales." . . . Scary!

BAD THING #5:
Taxpayers Pay for the Disaster

These big retail boxes take up a lot of a city's resources—streets, water, sewer lines, power tie-ins—and a lot of these services would have to be newly provided because Wal-Mart is, in its ideal plan, building on undeveloped property. You can bet, with Sam's eye on the bottom line, that he is not going to quietly pay for what he uses if he can stick it to somebody else. Indeed, the Portland *Oregonian* reported that when Wal-Mart opened its store in Lebanon, Oregon, "Things heated up at the city council when Wal-Mart 'suggested' the city make some improvements to its streets, water and sewer tie-ins, and add some traffic lights—a package that was estimated to cost a half-million dollars." This suggestion, remember, was from a discounter who was going to ship the dollars made in Lebanon right out of town the morning after, rarely pausing to invest a dime in the town that recently rolled out such a plush red carpet for it.

The Planning Board of New Paltz, New York, crunched

Local Law Enforcement Feels the Strain

When Wal-Mart comes to town, the local community also has to cough up the cost of the increased need for law enforcement. A number of small-town police departments have been speaking out about this unforeseen increase in their workload. Wal-Marts are almost always on the outskirts of their municipalities. And since the stores draw customers from a wider radius, the town's cops and courts are the ones who have to deal with the increased number of disturbances a big discount outlet attracts.

Harrisville, Utah (pop. 4,000) has felt the impact, according to a May 2004 AP report. Three years after a Supercenter opened on a former pasture outside of town, Harrisville police are fielding one-third more calls, the department has been forced to grow from four to six officers, and the court schedule has been extended to give the city prosecutor time to negotiate pleas. Patrol units monitor the parking lot, site of more than half of the depart-

some numbers on what would happen in their city (fiscally speaking) if they let Wal-Mart build a Supercenter in their town. Here are their enlightening findings:

Wal-Mart property tax	+$100,000
Cost of municipal services	−$29,000
Cost of additional services	−$5,000
Tax losses at three other malls	−$29,000
50 percent property tax abatement	−$50,000
Total town tax deficit	<$13,000>

ment's DUI investigations—in particular, late-night problems with methamphetamine users.

In the same story, Police Chief Bill Chilson of nearby Clinton recalled asking officers in towns that already had a Wal-Mart what to expect. "They laughed at me," he said. A judge from another town asked him, "Have you been Wal-Mart-ized yet?"

In West Sadsbury, Pennsylvania (pop. 2,444), Police Chief John Slauch reported "a significant increase in crime and incident calls for service from the day Wal-Mart opened." Crime jumped 55 percent between the year before Wal-Mart opened and 2003; calls for service increased 57 percent from 2002 to 2003. "It is at times overwhelming," says Slauch, adding that municipal taxes don't cover the extra costs to the eight-officer police force. "I really don't think Wal-Mart is concerned with what happens on the local level; they're concerned with how much money they're making. They're not looking at the burden they're creating."

At this conservative estimate, the town would actually come out losing $13,000 a year. This does not even begin to account for other losses brought about by stores closing, people losing their jobs, and the flight of local cash right back to Bentonville. You may not be surprised to learn that New Paltz decided not to allow the proposed Wal-Mart in their town.

But it gets worse. In many, many cases, Wal-Mart manages to avoid paying property taxes, in part or altogether. It's generally done via a neat little deal whereby the retailer officially buys the parcel it needs, then sells it to a local entity, which leases it back to Wal-Mart.

In other cases, Wal-Mart gets a rebate on some or *all* of

Wheeling and Dealing

The tax bite on the town where a Wal-Mart *store* moves in is peanuts compared to the truly obscene giveaways that Wal-Mart extracts when it chooses a location for one of its mammoth *distribution centers.* Now you're talking millions.

In July 2004, the *Fort Worth Star-Telegram* described the deal that went down in Baytown, Texas, when Wal-Mart decided an old U.S. Steel property nearby would be just right for its new, biggest-ever distribution center. The retailer managed to finagle a huge tax subsidy from the state. The tale has all the familiar features of Wal-Mart's Standard Operating Procedure:

Super-secret backroom negotiations. And how! The editor and publisher of the local *Baytown Sun*—a person by the curiously apt name of Wanda Garner Cash, who also sits on the economic development foundation board—signed a confidentiality agreement, neatly censoring any coverage in the paper that townsfolk depend on for local news. And the city council and county commissioners approved spending nearly half a million dollars on infra-

those local sales taxes that are supposed to provide such a boost to the community, or convinces the locals to pay for part or all of the infrastructure (roads, traffic signals, utilities, and the like) needed to establish the new facility. And if the locals won't deliver, Wal-Mart threatens to walk.

This standard practice has been a dirty dark secret for far too long, but the truth is coming out. The Good Jobs First (GJF) organization did an exhaustive study of local and state

structure without even knowing who the company was or the size of the tax incentive.

Local and state governments selling their souls to the giant retailer. Wal-Mart will "sell" its new facility to the state's Permanent School Fund, which will then lease it back to Wal-Mart. Because the fund is tax-exempt, not a single cent of local property taxes will ever be collected (the warehouse alone is four million square feet), saving Wal-Mart nearly $2 million a year—*$55 million* over the lease term.

A high-and-mighty Wal-Mart threatening to pick up its toys and go home if it doesn't get its way. According to Mike Shields, director of the Baytown/West Chambers County Economic Development Foundation, Wal-Mart "told us they definitely would not come without the permanent school funding. I'm convinced they would have walked."

Critics say it's a sweetheart deal and Wal-Mart would have located there without the incentives. We say yer damn right: it's time local governments start showing some backbone and calling Wal-Mart's bluff.

subsidies that Wal-Mart demands in return for the *privilege* of having their area graced with a Wal-Mart store or distribution center. GJF's May 2004 report, titled "Shopping for Subsidies: How Wal-Mart Uses Taxpayer Money to Finance Its Never-Ending Growth," is a must-read. You can get the full report or a six-page executive summary on their website, www.goodjobsfirst.org. Here's the brief description GJF provides [our emphasis]:

> "The subsidies to Wal-Mart were not a good deal. There was not a significant sales tax generation and we lost a lot of mom-and-pop businesses."
>
> —*Mayor Pro Tem Gregory Pettis*, *Cathedral City, California. Quoted in "Shopping for Subsidies," Good Jobs First.*

In this extensively researched study, we show that the giant retailer has received more than *$1 billion* in economic development subsidies from state and local governments across the country. Taxpayers have helped finance not only Wal-Mart stores, but also the company's huge network of distribution centers, more than 90% of which have gotten subsidies.

Think about it. The Walton family owns *$90 billion* worth of Wal-Mart stock. The company pays its store "associates" poverty wages. It mercilessly pressures its suppliers to deliver the goods for rock-bottom prices—or else. Do you think Wal-Mart needs or deserves to be given *one single dollar*, let alone *one billion dollars* of taxpayer money?

It is now well known that Wal-Mart personnel managers routinely advise their underpaid employees to take advantage of public and private social services, such as food stamps, food banks, soup kitchens, and local health clinics for the indigent. This is yet another subsidy we, the taxpayers, provide to the richest and most powerful company on the planet.

Two final notes brighten this gloomy picture. First, not every town hands the loot over to Wal-Mart. In Killingly, Connecticut, a coalition with labor union backing rallied opposition against the state's planned giveaway of $45 million

The Wal-Mart Welfare State

In August 2004, the University of California at Berkeley Center for Labor Research and Education produced a report titled *Hidden Cost of Wal-Mart Jobs: Use of Safety Net Programs by Wal-Mart Workers in California*. It found that the presence of Wal-Mart stores in California, with the low wages and skimpy benefits it offers workers, creates a hidden cost to the state's taxpayers because many of those workers must rely on public safety net programs—such as food stamps, Medi-Cal, and subsidized housing—to make ends meet. The report's main findings are as follows:

★ Reliance by Wal-Mart workers on public assistance programs in California costs taxpayers an estimated $86 million annually: $32 million in health-related expenses and $54 million in other assistance.

★ The families of Wal-Mart employees in California utilize an estimated 40 percent more in taxpayer-funded health care than the average for families of all other large retail employees.

★ The families of Wal-Mart employees use an estimated 38 percent more in other (non–health care) public assistance programs (such as food stamps, Earned Income Tax Credit, subsidized school lunches, and subsidized housing) than the average for families of all large retail employees.

★ If other large California retailers adopted Wal-Mart's wage and benefits standards, it would cost [California] taxpayers an additional *$410 million a year* in public assistance to employees.

The report focused on California, but the authors noted that if their estimates were applied nationwide, public assistance to Wal-Mart workers could be costing taxpayers some *$2 billion a year*!

in tax credits plus negative environmental consequences. Wal-Mart abandoned the project.

Second, there are several cases in which Wal-Mart failed to hold up its end of the deal—and in at least one, the retailer was held accountable. For example, Streetsboro, Ohio, granted Wal-Mart enterprise-zone benefits, but when Wal-Mart didn't comply with its hiring commitments, the city council cut back on the promised benefits and eventually revoked them. Good to know that *someone* is holding the Benton-villains to their obligations.

BAD THING #6: Other Towns Suffer

It's not just towns that actually have a Wal-Mart within their city limits that feel the negative effects on their commerce and quality of life. But then again, that's all part of the plan. The sales area of a Wal-Mart is about seventy miles in diameter, and one of Wal-Mart's corporate strategies is to "carpet" the land—essentially, they want every settlement in the entire country to fall within the sales area of at least one Wal-Mart. So it stands to reason that a number of towns will lose commerce to a nearby Wal-Mart without getting much of anything in return. Take the author's hometown of Grand Saline, Texas (population 3,000).

In the '20s and '30s (and '40s and '50s and so on), a person had to actually search for a parking space downtown. Now it's almost empty—and it's even worse on Saturday, which used to be the busiest shopping day of the week. The city sales tax revenue dropped 54 percent over a twelve-month period. The First National Bank went out of business. Once there were three drug stores, three thriving dry goods stores, three stores selling appliances. Now: one, none, and none, respectively.

Grand Saline doesn't have a Wal-Mart, but Mineola and Canton—both only thirteen miles away—do. Grand Saline's

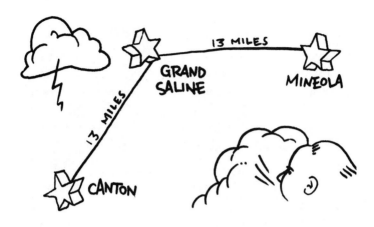

own businesses have sickened and died and its downtown has shriveled. Grand Saline is becoming a commercial suburb of the Wals in Mineola and Canton. It's hard to watch this happening to one's hometown!

BAD THING #7: Wal-Mart Moves On

Even scarier are the tales of woe from the towns that actually were strip-mined by Wal-Mart. A small town's lifeblood isn't always enough to feed the world's largest discounter—not anymore.

"Wal-Mart's Surge Leaves Dead Stores Behind." That's the headline on a September 2004 *Wall Street Journal* feature. As Wal-Mart replaces its original discount stores (you remember those puny 60,000-to-70,000-square-footers?) with 200,000-plus-square-foot Supercenters, the discount stores' empty hulks stand vacant in small towns across America. But Wal-Mart would have you believe that it works hard to find just the right tenant to replace it: "When we make the decision to relocate, our primary focus is to find a tenant for the building that suits the needs of the community."

Don't you believe 'em. The towns stuck with these eye-

Make Us an Offer!

Wal-Mart's real estate website, www. wal-martrealty.com, has become much more sophisticated since our second edition.

These days, as befits the nation's largest real estate developer, the up-front message is more businesslike.

> Wal-Mart Realty concentrates on commercial real estate located in or around our current and former locations.

But click the Economic Development tab to find that old warm and fuzzy message of yore:

> Wal-Mart Stores and Sam's Clubs are often so successful that they outgrow their buildings and relocate to better serve our customers. When this happens, Wal-Mart Realty looks for ways to help the community continue to prosper by offering these properties for sublease and/or sale. . . . It is our commitment to these communities and our shareholders to keep these buildings in productive use.

And under the heading "Community Values," the giant reassures us:

> When we make the decision to relocate, our primary focus is to find a tenant for the building that suits the needs of the community.

Awwww! And here we were, thinking their primary focus was to get the hell outta there, leaving behind the bleached carcass of an "obsolete" Wal-Mart—and a formerly thriving town.

sores sure don't. It turns out Wal-Mart generally blocks any of the obvious tenants—big-box retailers, that is—from taking over the facilities that were designed expressly for . . . big-box retail. When the article was published, Wal-Mart had about 152 vacant stores across the country—the equivalent of *13 million square feet*. One store, in Bardstown, Kentucky, sat forlorn for ten years before Wal-Mart was convinced to allow a flea market.

La Junta, Colorado, featured in the same *Wall Street Journal* piece, expanded its town boundaries to allow the original construction. Wal-Mart used the structure for fewer than ten years before abandoning it for a new Supercenter just a quarter of a mile away. Its lease on the vacant store runs through the year 2017.

Consider the story of Nowata, Oklahoma—brought down not once but twice by Wal-Mart's policies of expansion and consolidation.

Nowata is an oil town of about four thousand souls in north central Oklahoma. In 1982 Wal-Mart came to town and quickly became the "new downtown." According to an article in *The New York Times*, a collapse in world oil prices and the typically splashy opening of the superstore combined to drive roughly half the local shops out of business. For over ten years Wal-Mart was the city's biggest business and, with seventy employees, its second biggest employer.

Then, in 1994, Wal-Mart left, and the city of Nowata was shattered again. This was a town that had sacrificed its business diversity to the "box" and had quickly come to depend on the presence of Wal-Mart in town. The citizens of Nowata, disproportionately poor and elderly, loyally shopped at Wal-Mart, keeping its revenues healthy: An analysis of the store's sales tax payments in the early '90s shows that, on average, the residents of Nowata were spending over $1,200 a year per person at Wal-Mart. Bryan L. Lee, president of the First National Bank of Nowata, where Wal-Mart made night deposits, has said that daily receipts for the store were as strong and steady right before the store closed as they had ever been in the store's history.

So what happened? It seems the good citizens of Nowata—like those in a growing number of Wal-Mart towns across the country—got caught in the next phase of Wal-Mart's growth strategy: "consolidation." In short, the construction of a new Wal-Mart Supercenter in Bartlesville, thirty miles from Nowata, meant that two older and smaller Wal-Marts—the ones in Nowata and Pawhuska, to the south and east—had to go. And the folks who used to shop at those two smaller stores now had to travel to Bartlesville to get their tennis shoes and plastic tackle boxes.

For Nowata, Wal-Mart's pullout felt like disaster all over again. A lot of people were thrown out of work. Many folks who didn't have cars lost the only place where they could do some of their necessary shopping. And, due to lost sales tax, city officials were left scrambling to bridge an $80,000 deficit in the city's 1995 municipal budget of $1.2 million. To cope, city manager Nancy Shipley was forced to lay off some city workers, cancel projects, and raise taxes: water and sewer taxes climbed 32 percent.

More than anything, the town felt betrayed: Wal-Mart had come in, made itself necessary, then left without notice. Indeed, right before the store closed, Wal-Mart in Nowata posted signs outside: "The rumors are false: Wal-Mart will be here always." (When asked about these signs, Don E. Shinkle, Wal-Mart's vice president for corporate affairs, said that they were put up "based on market research at the time, and the later decision [to abandon the stores] was based on market research later." How's that for firm, reliable corporate policy?)

In some sense, you could say that this is the way things are: Businesses sometimes leave and deliver a crippling blow to the communities they abandon. This is part of the cost of doing business. But in a town like Nowata, cruelly cut down twice by the same massive retailer, that cost is too high, especially when it seems to be paid by the folks with the most to lose.

We Get Letters . . .

In the six or seven years since our first edition, we've received about two letters a week, many from employees or folks closely involved with the Wal-Mart operation. About a third of them asked that we not use their names—or even print the letter. But enough have given the OK for us to share their stories with you. . . .

Frank Greenly, manager of Shop'n Kart stores in Albany and Lebanon, Oregon, wrote in June 2002:

> We too are facing the onset of a Wal-Mart Supercenter. . . . It is in the preliminary stages at this point. After reading your book, I felt [it] could be a great tool in educating some key people in Lebanon on the negative effects on our small town. We've already seen the effects from the original Wal-Mart built here some ten years ago. Our downtown has been devastated. I would like to purchase twenty copies of your book to hand out. I hope you can help me in obtaining these books; I look forward to educating the people of Lebanon on the evils of those "blankety blanks."

We've checked for the latest in Lebanon. It ain't good, folks. And it's bad enough to learn that Wal-Mart had its way with Lebanon, but it's bitter indeed to find the news on a Wal-Mart website—walmart-oregon.com—that gloats "Construction has begun on Lebanon's new Wal-Mart Supercenter. . . . The Lebanon City Council agreed to a legal document filed by Wal-Mart that essentially grants approval of the new Supercenter's design plan. Also, the Oregon Court of Appeals recently rejected a legal appeal filed by those who oppose the new Supercenter."

Turns out Wal-Mart tore down one of the last drive-in movie theaters in the state to replace it with that Supercenter. The existing Lebanon Wal-Mart that Mr. Greenly mentions had to go too, of course. Only one Supercenter is needed to put local grocery stores out of business.

. . . And We Get Calls

We've been asked by civic groups in several cities to serve as a consultant, helping them keep a proposed Supercenter out of their area. These invitations would have been very tempting if we could have rolled back the age clock some twenty-five years! It's always a shot in the arm to hear from citizens out on the front lines. Even if their story ends in a Wal-Mart victory, we know there are now that many more sadder-but-wiser folks who've seen the ugly reality behind the smiley face—and who are spreading the word to others.

TWO SURE-FIRE WAYS WAL-MART BARGES INTO TOWN

(AND THREE WAYS IT SNEAKS IN)

Sam Walton claimed that one of his bedrock business principles was never to build in a town where Wal-Mart was not wanted. This was probably an easier thing to do way back in the day when Sam and Company were just beginning their pattern of world domination. Back then, towns didn't know what they were inviting in, and what Wal-Mart was selling sounded pretty good.

By the 1990s, things had definitely changed; dozens of private anti–Wal-Mart groups had sprung up throughout America. The majority are citizen activist groups in small towns where Wal-Mart has planned a store. The word is finally getting out about Wal-Mart's effect on a community, and the retailer is finding more and more towns that say, "We don't want you, Wal-Mart!"

But, in the words of New York developer John Nigro, who has worked to bring Wal-Mart into some of its targeted towns, "[the big retailers] know what they want." If Wal-Mart wants to come into your town, and it knows just where it wants a store to sit, Wal-Mart will come to town even when faced with a helluva fight.

BARGING IN WAY #1:
Location, Location, Location

To paraphrase the old real-estate saw about what makes a property desirable, there are really only three things Wal-Mart needs to move into a town:

(1) Zoning
(2) Zoning, and
(3) Zoning

The master plan for Wal-Mart, wherever it goes, involves the "box": the classic Wal-Mart square, prefab, ugly monstrosity of a building surrounded by asphalt parking lots as far as the eye can see. Uniform architecture is one of the keys to the retailer's scary success. No surprises; every place is the same. It's like mass production.

When Wal-Mart wants to come into a town, it fixes its eye on a certain parcel or parcels of land that will fit the bill: undeveloped and outside the downtown or other business district, with plenty of room for parking and easy access by the highway or other major roads.

Often, Wal-Mart will find its dream parcel, but it's not always zoned for the kind of heavy-duty retail use Wal-Mart wants it for. So Wal-Mart has to get the zoning changed before or at the same time that it applies for a business permit. Wal-Mart and its developers are pros at this and have prepared documents that show the city council and the planning commission that Wal-Mart will be the best imaginable new citizen of the town. (These proposals tend to be studded with what one Wal-Mart critic has dubbed "Wal-Math"; that is, "they only know how to add": more jobs, more community

Strike Three

I was delighted to see a *Bloomberg News* report that the Vermont Supreme Court turned down Wal-Mart's third attempt to put in a store in St. Albans, Vermont. The court said it "was proper for the state to consider the store's likely harm to competitors."

The court went a step beyond the above statement, ruling "that state law allowed the board to consider competition (like Wal-Mart's) as part of a project's impact on health, safety, and welfare. The closing of rival retailers would hurt local government's ability to raise taxes to provide services."

The dry (very dry) laugh I got from all this is in harking back to Wal-Mart founder Sam Walton's pledge that he would never put a store into a town where it was not wanted. Just think: Wal-Mart, after three rejections, was still trying to bully its way into St. Albans!

involvement, local buying, positive response to local needs—the whole phony-baloney ball of wax.)

It seems pretty clear that for people who don't want a Wal-Mart in their town, this is the best stage to stop it. The Lancaster County (Pennsylvania) Planning Commission put together a succinct summary of the steps small towns should take in "Wal-Mart-proofing" themselves. (Thanks, folks. This is dry stuff, but useful as hell.)

○ **Adopt urban growth boundaries.** In other words, limit the area in which urban-level development can happen within the town, and make those boundaries clear.

Don't Let This Happen to Your Town

In July 2004 in Centerville, Utah (a small bedroom community of Salt Lake City), the group Centerville Citizens First paid for a professional survey of local opinion about a proposed new Wal-Mart Supercenter—a 200,000-square-foot edifice on twenty-two acres at the gateway to the city, right next to a retirement residence. (Never mind that there were already ten Wal-Marts within twenty-two miles, including five Supercenters.) Surveyors from Insight Research of Salt Lake City interviewed four hundred town residents identified as heads of households, taking pains to ask balanced questions. A huge majority—73 percent—said they didn't want the superstore. Ray Briscoe of Insight Research said he had never experienced such intense feelings from survey respondents. For 96 percent of those interviewed, the Wal-Mart store was an important or very important issue.

The planning commission vote was a three-to-three deadlock, and Wal-Mart's plan was rejected. But the Centerville Board of Adjustment later reversed the decision. A commenter on the weblog "Utah Policymaker" wrote: "Centerville had ordinances on the books allowing for this type of development, and Wal-Mart has met those requirements. . . . If Centerville residents did not want this type of development, *they could and should have changed their zoning ordinance* long before Wal-Mart showed up and made an application." [our emphasis]

Words for every anti–Wal-Martian to read and heed!

- ✪ **Review local comprehensive plans.** A town's comprehensive plan is a document that sets out the goals and policies for a town's desired growth pattern. This is a town's statement of what it is and what it wants to become, and it can be a powerful document in fighting outside developers who have their own ideas about what should become of the town.

- ✪ **Review zoning ordinances.** A town's zoning ordinance should be consistent with the town's comprehensive plan.

- ✪ **Review subdivision and land development regulations.** These regulations specify what a developer must demonstrate about the nature and impact of its proposed development. Make sure the regulations are strong and detailed enough to give your town a clear picture of any proposed development—from the developer itself.

Many cities are crafting ordinances that effectively bar big-box chain stores, with requirements such as paying employees a living wage and a minimum level of benefits, not interfering with union efforts, and competing fairly with smaller retailers.

BARGING IN WAY #2: Put It on the Ballot

Foresighted citizens who work with their local governments to strengthen zoning laws can't rest on their laurels. Wal-Mart has the resources to draft ordinances and initiatives, then muster an army of paid signature-gatherers to place them on the ballot and bankroll a blitz of TV commercials, press releases, and slick mailers.

In June 2003 in Contra Costa County, California, the Board of Supervisors, responding to a wide range of constituents, passed an ordinance banning certain big-box stores (over ninety thousand square feet) from unincorporated parts of the county. Wal-Mart didn't even have any immediate plans to open a store there (at least, so the company claimed), but this was one line in the sand the Bentonville bullies just could not leave uncrossed. They mounted a petition and amassed enough signatures in support of "consumer choice" to place the ordinance on the ballot as Measure L in March 2003. A majority of "No" votes would repeal the ordinance.

Measure L's supporters—a coalition of residents, open-space proponents, labor unions, and the Safeway supermarket chain, calling itself the Neighborhood Alliance for Local Control—mustered $300,000 for its Yes on L campaign.

But Wal-Mart created its own "local" citizens' group, "Contra Costa Consumers for Choice." The retailer—er, that is, Contra Costa Consumers for Choice—spent over $1 million on TV spots and mailers to defeat Measure L. And a Wal-Mart spokeswoman declared ominously, "If we are successful, I would hope other communities take a long, hard look before passing ordinances that restrict consumer choice."

We're sorry to report that Measure L was voted down. Wal-Mart won.

But close on the heels of that defeat came a more heartening outcome elsewhere in California. When the Inglewood City Council said "No" to Wal-Mart's proposed sixty-acre Supercenter complex, Wal-Mart wrote its own seventy-one-page ballot initiative 04-A, which would have exempted the retailer from every single Inglewood planning, zoning, and environmental regulation. (Opponents pointed out that Wal-Mart paid its signature gatherers more than it pays its average clerk!) Again, Wal-Mart spent $1 million to blitz voters with its "free choice" message. Its community affairs spokesman said, "If organized labor and those elected officials they

Them That Has the Gold, Rules

When you rally your friends and neighbors to defeat a Wal-Mart initiative, beware of Wal-Mart's ties to local politicians.

According to www.sprawl-busters.com, Wal-Mart made $50,000 contributions to the campaigns of candidates running for city council and mayor of the town of Antioch in Contra Costa County, California, where Wal-Mart managed to get a local control ordinance voted down in 2003. The *Contra Costa Times* estimated that Wal-Mart would spend several million dollars in contributions to California electoral campaigns.

It seems that when you're the world's biggest and richest corporation, elections are yours for the buying. We're just going to have to work that much harder to beat Wal-Mart back.

put into power think they're going to attack Wal-Mart, then they better expect Wal-Mart to fight back."

But in April 2004, Inglewood voters spoke. A 61-percent majority soundly defeated Wal-Mart's attempt to dictate its will to a mere city government.

Like we said, it's not so easy anymore for Wal-Mart to just waltz into a town with its usual bag of tricks. The words "Wal-Mart is coming" are like a red flag for lots of citizens who have seen the havoc the monster retailer has wreaked in other towns. Townspeople are finding good ways to meet the threat by putting up websites for their campaigns, spreading the word locally, and networking with other communities who've won, lost, or are facing a similar battle.

But Wal-Mart isn't backing off so easily. Rather than do the right thing and say, "Oh, okay, small town, you don't want us, so we'll go elsewhere," it has thought up ways to get around those defenses. We've pinpointed three sleazy ways Wal-Mart weasels its way into your town—all just as sneaky as can be.

SNEAKY WAY #1:
Manipulate Existing Zoning

In Virginia, Wal-Mart was able to come up with an absolutely ingenious way to get around not one, but two sets of municipal codes at once. Here's what happened. In the town of Warrenton, the city code said that any retail outlet over fifty thousand square feet had to have special permission to be built. When the Wal came to Warrenton, it had to ask for such permission to put in its proposed monster: a 120,000-square-foot box. Properly alarmed at the thought, the city said "No," that's just too big for us. On the face of it, Wal-Mart was beat: they asked and got turned down.

Now, Fauquier County, which surrounds the town of Warrenton, has a similar code on its books, stating that retail

---

Here's Your Hat—What's Your Hurry?

In one county, the discounter wanted to take over a mobile home park occupied by 170 residents so it could build a 136,000-square-foot Supercenter. The company's original offer to the residents if they'd relocate? Two hundred big old American dollars. "This isn't fair," said one resident who had lived on the site for four and a half years. No, my friend, it's not.

Dateline North Carolina

T. R. Taylor and his wife wanted a house away from downtown that they could settle in for life. They found the perfect spot back in 1940—a one-and-a-half-acre wooded plot. They built their house and cleared some trees to make a garden. Decades went by before their dreams were shattered. A Wal-Mart was built around them, ruining the property they had been on for sixty years. Wal-Mart bought the land next to theirs and bulldozed around their house, leaving them twenty feet up a bank, with a ditch thirty feet across and three hundred feet long separating their property from the superstore. An insulting offer was made for the Taylors' property—an offer that they turned down. Even the line of trees that was supposed to buffer the house from the development never materialized. The Taylors' son sums it up thusly: "Human beings do not do this to other human beings."

outlets exceeding seventy-five thousand square feet have to be approved.

But voila! Wal-Mart found an appropriately zoned parcel that straddled the line between Warrenton and unincorporated Fauquier County, and the discounter was able to get around both sets of restrictions by putting less than fifty thousand square feet of its box inside Warrenton land, and less than seventy-five thousand square feet on Fauquier County land! Local courts found that the use was permitted—or at least was not excluded—by the available laws.

Thirteen neighbors of the proposed Wal-Mart development appealed the ruling. One of them, Deborah Gortenhuis, said in an interview with the *Washington Post,* "I think it's sort of sneaky that they want to do this thing. Wal-Mart tries to depict itself as this very honest, family-oriented, small-town kind of store. But with all this sneaking around, you wonder about that. It seems ruthless." We couldn't have said it better ourselves.

SNEAKY WAY #2: Use a Front Man

This is a damned effective technique. From what we can see, it's one of Wal-Mart's favorites. Check it out.

Some aware citizens in Evergreen, Colorado, suspected that Wal-Mart was scoping out their town for a possible location. They called Wal-Mart headquarters several times and asked them what its development plans were for Evergreen. Each time the reply was the same: "We are not looking at real estate in Evergreen."

Meanwhile, a real estate development company from Denver appeared before the county zoning board, asking for rezoning on a couple of parcels. They don't own the parcels, but are interested in getting them rezoned, then acquiring them for later sale or lease to Wal-Mart. In this way, the path will be paved for Wal-Mart to come in, and local citizens who would wish to keep it out have lost one of their most powerful weapons in the fight: strict zoning restrictions.

We heard that the city council of Ithaca, New York, unanimously voted to spend $3,600 in outside lawyer fees to keep Wal-Mart from building a store just inside the city limits. Seems a development company from South Carolina, working on Wal-Mart's behalf, had secured a conditional zoning variance from the city to build "an unidentified store." When the city found out the store was to be a Wal-Mart, they said "No." And the citizens' group Stop Wal-Mart managed to hold off the company even when Wal-Mart sued through the courts.

Let this be a warning to would-be Wal-Mart busters: Keep an eye on rezoning requests that would make a parcel Wal-Mart-ready, no matter who has submitted the request. You never know who's really behind it.

SNEAKY WAY #3: Hell, Use a Straw Man

In our first edition, we had found only one example of Wal-Mart using this particular tactic, but apparently it's working for the Bentonvillains, because they've continued to use it. After all, it's become a popular strategy for political candidates to send election-time mailers supposedly from a "concerned citizens' group." Many voters seem to fall for these; they're too busy or distracted to look for the fine print.

Here's a more recent example: When Wal-Mart mounted its expensive (and ultimately successful) campaign to defeat a Contra Costa County, California, ban on certain big-box stores in unincorporated areas ("Barging In Way #2"), a new local organization surfaced: "Contra Costa Consumers for Choice." Their claim? That the board was denying consumers freedom of choice. And who were they? Why, just your friends and neighbors who would be grievously injured by the lack of a big-box retailer selling groceries on the outskirts of town. The fine print at the bottom of their letterhead? "Paid for by Contra Costa Consumers for Choice with major funding provided by Wal-Mart Stores, Inc."

We Get Letters . . .

IN GALENA, WAL-MART GETS THE STORE BUT NOT THE SUBSIDY

In February 2003, we received a letter from Dick Hartig. He's CEO of America's second oldest continuously operated family drug chain, Hartig Drug Stores, with stores in Iowa, Illinois, and Wisconsin. The company just celebrated its one-hundred-year anniversary in 2004. But at the store in Galena, Illinois, the celebration was bittersweet. . . .

Dear Bill:

I would like to write to you my "whole story" as you suggest on page 169, but heck . . . I'd have to write a whole book about the size of yours to do justice to my saga.

I'm a third-generation pharmacist, fifty-three years old, with a wife and two great high school boys at home. I spend about half of my time battling Wal-Mart in some way, shape, or form every day. In a nutshell, I've lost one store to Wal-Mart, and they're after me again. About three years ago, I located a piece of land in Illinois's oldest and most historic city, Galena. The city's claim to fame is that it was home to General Ulysses S. Grant.

I finally got the store built in 2000. You can see the store on my web page (www.hartigdrug.com). Great-looking drugstore, all humility aside. Wal-Mart decided I had picked a pretty good spot, so they rode into town

The Wal-Mart Wriggle

Chain Store Age magazine mulled over Wal-Mart's defeat in an article titled "The Lessons of Inglewood" (May 2004). Retailers were advised to watch out for a growing trend of resistance to the big boxes: For example, a number of municipalities, hoping to stem the invasion of megamarkets and warehouse clubs, have passed new regulations limiting the entry of stores bigger than one hundred thousand square feet that draw over 10 percent of sales from food items.

Would this stop Wal-Mart, or could it find a way to wriggle under the bar? Those wise to the mega-retailer's ways can guess the answer. Yep, Wal-Mart has whipped up a prototype design for a smaller Supercenter. Precisely ninety-nine thousand square feet.

and told the City they needed two million bucks in tax abatement and forgivable grants to do the City a favor and build a Supercenter. A referendum was held, and resoundingly the community said "No" to any assistance. Tail between their legs, [Wal-Mart] whimpered off promising never to return.

Alas, seven months later they were back! This time, however, they weren't looking for any "help" per se, just a revision of the plat that would allow them to obliterate and dilute my "100 percent corner" lot. Craftily, they didn't use the term "rezoning," although that is in fact what they were after. I filed a written petition as the adjacent landowner, forcing a supermajority vote by the Council. It passed four to three and I filed suit. After the suit was filed, Wal-Mart came in and bought the land (sixteen acres) for a million bucks. (I had paid just shy of $400,000 for my two acres.) By buying, they established their "interest" in the outcome of my suit and sent an army of lawyers to Galena. I haven't stepped foot in a courtroom as I write, but I have managed to drop more than $20,000 on legal [fees] to date.

It's lonely fighting these guys, and I feel like any friend I can get is a friend I desperately need. Your book was uplifting and conciliatory. If you know of any resources I can tap as I move forward, I'd be grateful.

We called Mr. Hartig and had a good conversation. But late in 2004 we learned the sad outcome. After pleading his case for nearly three years with the developer, the City of Galena, and Wal-Mart, that cost him hundreds of hours of work and significant legal expense, Hartig had settled his case out of court. Wal-Mart's new Supercenter was slated to open, directly behind the handsome Hartig Drug Store, in January 2005.

We've read the news stories, and what happened to Mr. Hartig sure smells fishy to us. When he bought his property, he studied the zoning very carefully. The preliminary plat for a planned unit development called for a mixture of commercial, residential, and multifamily plots. He paid a premium for his two-acre front corner parcel. Then Wal-Mart came along and with one council vote, the zoning was amended (er, the plat was revised) to give them the entire remaining sixteen acres. Mr. Hartig's argument that this was plain wrong fell on deaf ears.

Although in the end the city council was wooed and won by Wal-Mart, we are heartened by one feature of Mr. Hartig's ordeal. When the council first balked at handing Wal-Mart a $2 million sales tax rebate to locate there, Wal-Mart lowered its demand to $1.5 million. And when Wal-Mart warned them it would walk if the town didn't fork over that $1.5 million, the good folks of Galena called Wal-Mart's bluff! Despite the usual Wal-Mart campaign (full-page ads on why to vote for the Supercenter), even voters who said they'd like to have a Wal-Mart store said they shouldn't have to subsidize the world's largest company. A newspaper editorial was headlined "Wal-Mart Welcome—At Its Own Expense." Fifty-seven percent of voters said "No" to the subsidy, and the council followed the will of the public, refusing to allow Wal-Mart the tax break.

We hope all you anti-Wal-Martians in the greater Galena area will take your business to Hartig Drug.

3

TWO WAYS WAL-MART IS OH SO GREEDY

Greed is the driver in two of Wal-Mart's sorriest practices: the crummy way they treat their workers, and the cold-hearted, iron-fisted way they squeeze their suppliers. Let's tackle 'em in that order.

GREEDY WAY #1:
Employees Are Wrung Dry

Of all the things wrong with Wal-Mart, the one that most people have finally caught wind of is the crummy way they treat their workers, especially the front-line "associates" who run the stores and distribution centers. Wal-Mart knows that we know, but how have they responded? Just as you'd expect from the likes of them. Rather than change their policies, they've launched a huge, expensive self-defense campaign to "educate" the public. Maybe you've seen those warm and fuzzy commercials featuring beaming "associates" who confide how much they LO-O-O-OVE working at Wal-Mart—it's like one big happy family!

Chintziness Personified

We got a kick out of a Wal-Mart spokesman telling a reporter why Wal-Mart's annual managers' meeting had to be split in two.

Fifteen thousand managers are required to attend an annual preview of holiday merchandise and management presentations. The conference alternates between Dallas and Houston, and neither of those big cities has enough *low-priced* rooms to house all 15,000. So one group of 7,500 shows up on Saturday and Sunday; the following Tuesday and Wednesday the other 7,500 attend.

In plain Wal-Mart language: "Always the lowest-priced room. Always."

INSIDE THE BEAST

For the first edition, we conducted an interview with a former Wal-Mart manager: a man who had been on the inside of the beast for over fifteen years. A lot of what Joe (not his real name) had to say speaks to the top Two Ways Wal-Mart Is Oh So Greedy. And from everything we read and hear, the conditions Joe described back then have not changed.

BQ: Joe, your wife tells me your hours as a manager were so long you barely knew your children?

Joe: Long hours were demanded—rarely less than seventy a week, most weeks eighty or more. Days off were rare. And I have gone as long as three years without a vacation. My wife literally raised our children by herself.

BQ: Hourly workers, I've been told, are held to a minimum?

Joe: You won't believe how they are treated. Managers try to

keep employees' hours under twenty-eight a week so they won't be eligible for benefits.

If business slows on any day, managers are instructed to send workers home anytime after they have four hours on the clock. Even department heads who are supposed to be regulars can be sent home, often working less than the eight hours they are entitled to.

BQ: This is a personal question, and you may not want to answer it. But how much did you make as a store manager?

Joe: You'll laugh at this. But before I quit in the 1980s, I made $15,000 a year, but I could draw up to $15,000 against my annual bonus, which I normally had to do. Most I ever made was $35,000. And I was considered one of their better managers, constantly on the upgrade, getting better stores.

BQ: When you moved, did Wal-Mart pay your expenses?

Joe: No. Actually, the "system" was to ask store personnel to do you a favor by working off the clock to come out to your place and help you pack. You were moved to your next assignment, always, in a Wal-Mart truck. And at your new station you asked for volunteers to come out and help you un-pack. Never on company time. Always off the clock.

BQ: What about real estate you might leave behind?

Joe: Wal-Mart headquarters always bluntly told you they were not in the real estate business. Had never been. Would never be. And, on our next-to-last move, we took a helluva loss on our home.

BQ: Suppose you told your regional manager you were happy where you were and didn't want to move?

Joe: That wouldn't work either. It was always a larger store, paying a little more. But in spite of that, I told my boss one time I wanted to stay where I was. Then I got a call from the vice president of stores from my area to suggest, in the strongest terms, that I start packing. It was as simple as that. If I refused, I was out the door, fired, through with my future at Wal-Mart.

Why didn't I quit? I've asked myself that a thousand times. But one gets to doing something, knows he's good at it, and feels, ultimately, that things will get a lot better. I don't know why I didn't get the hell out sooner, but when you've got a family and lots of years invested, you just stay with the company.

BQ: I've heard that when you had annual meetings to which your wife was invited, they wouldn't allow you to use your own car?

Joe: That's another not-so-funny joke. I remember a couple of those widely touted "family" affairs the company called "Wal-Mart Ballyhoos." Always by bus.

Four or five managers would drive their own cars to a central Wal-Mart store, load up, travel on to the next central pick-up point, pick up another group, and so on until the bus was loaded to the gills. We went up to one meeting in Missouri that was a fourteen-hour bus drive. Got up at 5:00 A.M.

to catch the bus. No stop for lunch. And, everyone was required to bring their own sack snacks. Once there . . . tired, tired, tired . . . no refreshment bar.

Then two days of intense meetings, 7:00 A.M. until almost midnight. Then, on the fourth day, back on that damn bus for home. And on that fifth day, you had better be back to work—on time.

On another of these trips they said it would be at the rather nice Hot Springs Majestic Hotel. Not for us. It was something like a Day's Inn, and a long, long walk to the Majestic, where our meetings were held.

BQ: I've heard awful stories about how mean Wal-Mart can be to its vendors.

Joe: That's one of the reasons I had to quit. I had one lady whose main job was to make claims of product damage, or claim that the full order was not received, pallet damage, whatever. The company's policy was to make a vendor prove the full order was sent. On damage, they had to believe our claim—or lose Wal-Mart as a customer. You can't believe the number of claims an average Wal-Mart store makes in a single year. Not one store. All stores.

BQ: What about local vendors?

Joe: When we bought from a local vendor, except for utilities, of course, we were instructed to deduct 10 percent. Don't ask me for what. If we had to call in someone to service something, same thing. Quite often the invoice would be held up if there was the slightest question. Normally, the local vendor would allow us to take the 10 percent. I was against all this— to the fullest. But those were our instructions.

BQ: When you finally quit Wal-Mart, were you fully vested?

Joe: I thought so. I calculated I had $30,000 coming. But you can't believe the deductions they added to my final check. Administrative expenses, deductions I never dreamed of. The final amount was only $5,000. I should have sued, but that would have entailed legal expense, and like all claims against Wal-Mart, it would have been in the courts forever.

BQ: What was your actual reason for quitting?

Joe: My conscience was eating me up. My normal weight is around two hundred pounds, and I was down to about 145. My deepest concern was that I was selling out every moral I ever believed in.

BQ: Would you say Wal-Mart is dishonest?

Joe: I don't know how to answer that. I do know they take advantage of virtually everybody who has ever worked for them. I do know that they take every advantage of their vendors. I do know that they take advantage of every customer who walks into their store.

My greatest regret in life is that I ever tied up with Wal-Mart in the first place. And I know in my heart that if you interviewed every former manager of Wal-Mart, the vast majority of them would tell you an almost identical story [to this one] I'm telling you today.

Sadly, Joe is right; his story is not unique. Many Wal-Mart employees (er, "associates") are honorable, capable, hardworking folks. It's too bad their big boss pretty much sees them as bumps on his bottom line.

It is widely acknowledged that one of the great keys to Wal-Mart's formidable success is its lower-than-low cost of doing business. Wages in particular are as low as can be. Of the hundreds of places Wal-Mart can (and does!) save money, its workers' hides are the favorite.

Minimum wages and minimum benefits: that's the way Wal-Mart stays ultracompetitive. Here are a few more "features" of working for the world's largest retailer.

LOW PAY, SCANTY HOURS

According to the U.S. Census Bureau, retail jobs pay the least of all categories of employment: lower than service, lower than mining, certainly lower than manufacturing. A full-time retail wage normally puts the earner well below the federal poverty line. So the people who work at Wal-Mart are not looking at the rosiest picture to start with.

Then it gets worse. According to the August 2004 report by the University of California, Berkeley, California Labor Center, "Hidden Cost of Wal-Mart Jobs":

Meet the New Boss—Same as the Old Boss

Since our second edition, it's become public knowledge that Wal-Mart, the United States' largest private employer, is an absolute Scrooge with a workforce of struggling Bob Cratchits. It's gotten so when the mega-retailer tries to muscle its way into a new territory, that ol' "Great jobs are coming!" propaganda just doesn't fly anymore. For some reason, more and more people say they don't want to shop where the help has to be on some kind of public assistance to make ends meet.

So, starting in June 2004, Bentonville began implementing a new pay structure. As reported in *Business Week*, "associates" would be sorted into seven pay classes, each with a starting and top rate. Fixed raise amounts were set: satisfactory workers would get a forty-cent-an-hour boost, "above standard" workers, fifty-five cents.

Good news for "associates"? Not really. It was bad news, certainly, for long-time employees who've hung in there, watching their wages inch upward at a snail's pace,

Wal-Mart workers in California earn on average 31 percent less than workers employed in large retail as a whole, receiving an average wage of $9.70 per hour compared to the $14.01 average hourly earnings for employees in large retail (firms with 1,000 or more employees). . . . The differences are even greater when Wal-Mart workers are compared to unionized grocery workers. In the San Francisco Bay Area, non-managerial Wal-Mart employees earn on average $9.40 an hour, compared to $15.31 for unionized grocery workers. . . .

if at all. Under the old system you got your raise as a percentage, so the higher your current wage, the bigger the increase would be. Under the new system, the more you were making, the smaller your percentage increase would be.

Say you're a first-year "associate" making $8.00 an hour; a forty-cent raise is a decent 5 percent (whether $8.40 an hour is a decent wage is another story). But for the seasoned coworkers in your "class" who are making, say, $11.00, forty cents is just 3.6 percent. How's that for rewarding loyal service? Plus, now there's a cap on how much you can make in your "class." And a store can give no more than one in twenty of its workers an annual merit raise.

Wal-Mart, of course, spun this new scheme to their workers as "just like a union contract."

Says an organizer for the United Food and Commercial Workers (UFCW) organizer: "In the long term, [the plan] will cost [Wal-Mart] less" as senior, higher-paid workers get discouraged and leave.

Remember that many Wal-Marters work part-time (the company doesn't release employment data, so we don't know how many). Now realize that Wal-Mart defines "full-time" as twenty-eight hours per week or more, and you'll see a workforce where the actual majority does not work a regular, forty-hour work week at all.

THE DISPOSABLE WORKER

Even "full-time" Wal-Mart workers have no job security: none, zippo, zero. As first reported in an article in *Inc.* magazine's July 1994 issue, regular employees are subject to having their hours cut any time, any hour of the day, whenever business slows down. Managers are under pressure to keep staff levels in line with the flow of business, and often this is done on the fly, right in the middle of a shift. Makes it a little hard to plan the old household budget, doesn't it?

And if business overall slows down? Well, in the words of one of its suppliers' reps, Wal-Mart operates on the basis of sink or swim; and it doesn't care if you sink. Just keep hoping that Bentonville HQ doesn't shut down your whole store.

ROTTEN BENEFITS

When Wal-Mart personnel managers recruit eager new employees, they make much of the company's benefits.

How good are they? Not very, according to our calculations.

Let's take retirement—the 401(k) plan. According to the *Wall Street Journal*, a survey found that "Wal-Mart stores reallocate forfeitures to remaining plan participants." This means that some contributions originally destined to aid young, lower-paid employees end up benefiting longer-service, higher-paid employees.

At Wal-Mart, for example, it takes seven years for an employee to become fully vested (that is, entitled to the employer's contributions). That's the maximum period allowed by law for a graded vesting schedule. (By way of comparison, at our old company, Quinn Publications, employees were vested after one year.)

In his *Frontline* interview in 2004, former Wal-Mart manager Jon Lehman said worker compensation had deteriorated since the passing of Mr. Sam. Before that time, the profit-sharing plan helped make some of the original "associates" millionaires. (We do hope that those millionaires are now philanthropists, shifting some of that fortune back into the pockets of the needy who toiled to help create it.) But, says Lehman, "You won't make that today. The profit-sharing program . . . is a token plan. [They say to "associates"] 'We still partner with you. . . . We want to share the profits. Make sure you don't use too many light bulbs or too much floor wax. [This] will help your profits.'"

After lousy wages, the second most notorious aspect of Wal-Mart's inadequate worker compensation must be its equally lousy health-care coverage. A September 2003 *Wall Street Journal* article, "Wal-Mart Cost-Cutting Finds a Big Target in Health Benefits," honors Wal-Mart with the distinction of setting an "industry benchmark" for lowest health-care benefits. Only about half of its workforce has coverage because many don't work enough hours to meet Wal-Mart's minimum for inclusion. But out of those who do, only 60 percent sign up compared to 72 percent with other retailers. The other 40 percent probably take a look at Wal-Mart's high premiums, high deductibles (much higher than the industry average), and restrictions on care, and say "The heck with it."

Analysts estimate that in 2003 the stingy retailer spent an average of $3,500 per covered employee—almost 40 per-

Workers Pay for Health Care—
and Wal-Mart Profits

According to the UFCW's "Wal-Mart Bull Buster" fact sheet, Wal-Mart has increased the health-care premium cost for its workers by over 200 percent since 1993—during a period in which medical care inflation was only 50 percent. Wal-Mart is actually taking more from its workers than it needs to cover those cost increases.

cent less than the average for all U.S. corporations and 30 percent less than other U.S. wholesale/retail companies. It won't pay for smart preventive-care treatments such as flu shots, children's vaccinations, chiropractic, or eye exams. New full-time hires have to wait six months for coverage and a full year for treatment of pre-existing conditions; part-timers wait a full two years. With the high turnover at Wal-Mart, chances are fifty-fifty that a worker will be gone before they're even eligible. Compare that with Costco employees, who become eligible after three months (full-time) or six months (part-time).

When you hear Wal-Mart CEO Scott boast, as he did in 2004, of the "almost $2 billion" the company would spend on health-care benefits that year, just keep in mind how many workers those dollars must cover. Based on 500,000 employees, that's less than $4,000 each. The retail industry average is $4,894; the corporate average, $5,646. (And we wonder where Mr. Scott gets that $2 billion figure; in 2003 Wal-Mart spent $1.3 billion on 537,000 covered workers—that's a measly $2,421 each!)

Maybe you're thinking that health-care insurance pre-

Wal-Mart Bankrolls a Defeat in California

In November 2004, Californians voted on Proposition 72, a statewide initiative that would have required big employers, such as Wal-Mart, to either offer adequate, affordable health-care coverage to all of its employees or contribute to a state insurance fund. You can bet that Wal-Mart dipped into its war chest to fund the campaign against Proposition 72. Its position: "Wal-Mart believes companies should have the opportunity to provide benefit choices that both they and their employees can afford."

It pains us to relate that California voters rejected Prop. 72, 50.9 percent to 49.1 percent.

miums for *everyone* have been skyrocketing for some years now; so aren't *all* employers cutting back on health-care coverage? Not so. In 2003, 13 percent did reduce benefits, but 7 percent expanded them. That's across the board; but in the retail industry, said one of the consultants for the article, "You've got to benchmark constantly what your competition is doing [and] you certainly want to benchmark to Wal-Mart."

Wal-Mart: once again leading the race to the bottom.

And who makes up the difference? Why, you and me, the taxpayers, of course. Wal-Mart workers must rely on public assistance, far more than other retail employees. Former Wal-Mart manager Jon Lehman put it this way:

> I had a Rolodex on my desk . . . full of business cards of social service outfits in the local city . . . organizations that provided indigent health care, soup kitchens, every-

Nickel and Dimed

For any true anti-Wal-Martian, a must-read book is Barbara Ehrenreich's *Nickel and Dimed: On (Not) Getting By in America*. Ehrenreich worked for a month as a Wal-Mart "associate," and the chapter in her book about this experience offers some of her most biting commentary:

> For sheer grandeur, scale, and intimidation value, I doubt if any corporate orientation exceeds that of Wal-Mart. I have been told that the process will take eight hours, which will include two fifteen-minute breaks and one half-hour break for a meal, and will be paid for like a regular shift. . . . In orientation, we learned that the store's success depends entirely on us, the associates; in fact, our bright blue vests bear the statement "At Wal-Mart, our people make the difference." Underneath those vests, though, there are real-life charity cases, maybe even shelter dwellers.

Ehrenreich wonders, "Why does anybody put up with the wages we're paid?" When a hotel workers' strike raises the union issue, Ehrenreich begins cautiously talk-

thing, the United Way—all these people that I had lined up that I would call in the event that an associate came into my office and said, "I can't afford to take my child to the doctor," "I can't afford groceries," or "I'm getting kicked out of my house," or whatever. And I would actually call these places. Many times, I would take the worker down to the United Way in my truck.

ing about the need for one with her fellow "associates,"
and

> I soon become a walking repository of complaints.
> No one gets paid overtime at Wal-Mart, I'm told,
> though there's often pressure to work it. Many feel
> the health insurance isn't worth paying for. . . . my
> favorite subject, which is the abysmal rate of pay,
> seems to be a painful one. . . . one woman says
> "They talk about having spirit, but they don't give
> us any reason to have any spirit."

And finally, on the brink of shedding her blue "associate"
vest and walking out, she observes,

> Someone has to puncture the prevailing fiction that
> we're a "family" here, we "associates" and our "ser-
> vant leaders," held together solely by our commit-
> ment to the "guests." After all, you'd need a lot
> stronger word than *dysfunctional* to describe a fam-
> ily where a few people get to eat at the table while
> the rest—the "associates" and all the dark-skinned
> seamstresses and factory workers worldwide who
> make the things we sell—lick up the drippings from
> the floor: *psychotic* would be closer to the mark.

They didn't know what to do. I'd take them down, help
them make [an] application and get some help, you
know. . . .

I thought I was doing a good thing at the time.
Now when I look back, I think, "Wow, that's incredibly
poor that the company doesn't care enough about its
workers to pay them a living wage and to help them

with their medical costs, to pay for their medical expenses and things like that."

It's no wonder that so many Wal-Mart employees must look elsewhere for their health-care coverage. Wal-Mart freely admits that a goodly portion of their employees get their health-care benefits from a spouse or the state or federal government.

Think about it. By handing off the expense of providing health insurance to over 500,000 of its employees—to responsible employers and taxpayers—Wal-Mart benefits to the tune of $1 billion annually, according to the United Food and Commercial Workers (UFCW).

Speaking of the UFCW, many of the folks who work at the big grocery chains are card-carrying members. So Wal-Mart's Supercenter invasion—with its direct threat to the grocers, and all those underpaid "associates" who toil without union protection—has been like a red flag waved in front of the union's nose. The chains argue that they can't compete with Wal-Mart unless they slash their expenses to match those "low prices."

Now, the UFCW recently surveyed grocery shoppers in Colorado and Washington state, and 85 percent said they believe that the major supermarkets there—like Albertsons, Kroger, and Safeway—were very profitable and have a responsibility to provide workers with affordable health-care benefits. Will those shoppers keep shopping at those stores after Wal-Mart arrives and tries to lure them with cheaper food—shelved, rung up, and bagged by folks who can't afford to pay the premiums for the health care Wal-Mart offers?

WAL-MART WORKERS—VICTORIES AT LAST?

In our second edition, we told the hopeful tale of a battle won in Jacksonville, Texas.

Maurice Miller, a forty-five-year-old meat cutter, got tired of making $11 an hour at this grueling job when union meat cutters at Kroger stores in the area were making $14.66 an hour, $13.29 for apprentices—plus paid health insurance, dental insurance, and vision care. When a promised raise didn't come through, Miller turned to the UFCW in Grapevine, Texas, for help.

Organizer Brad Edwards knew what he was up against when he took up the fight: not a single Wal-Mart in the U.S. was unionized—let alone in East Texas.

All ten full-time meat market workers were declared eligible to vote. And they chose to unionize, seven to three.

A gigantic 70 percent victory! A clear win for the unions. Hope was in the air.

But Wal-Mart, true to its anti-union past, found a way out. It shut down the meat-cutting department and fired them all—a clear violation of the National Labor Relations Act (NLRA), the federal law that guarantees the right to organize. The National Labor Relations Board (NLRB) ordered Wal-Mart to reopen the department, hire back the workers, and bargain with the union. Wal-Mart appealed. As we go to press, the case is still undecided. But even if found guilty, Wal-Mart can be held accountable only for restoring the lost pay of fired workers (generally a few thousand dollars, tops), no matter how many times the company has violated the Act.

So our hopes turn north of the border—to Canada— and to the other side of the globe—China.

Canadian labor law makes the path to a union less rocky. Provinces have more of a say in this than the individual U.S. states do, and some provinces are more union-friendly than others. As we pen this, the UFCW is working with Wal-Mart employees who want to unionize stores in five provinces: British Columbia, Manitoba, Ontario, Quebec, and Saskatchewan. And it's been quite a roller coaster ride, with some workers voting for a union, Wal-Mart fighting back with their usual challenges, and Canadian courts and labor boards standing up (so far) for the workers.

In Saguenay, north of Quebec City, Wal-Mart challenged the unionization vote, claiming more workers were eligible than had voted. The labor board tossed out this challenge and ordered the retailer to meet with the union to begin negotiating an agreement. Stay tuned. . . .

The union victory at the Jonquiere, Quebec, store was especially heartening. In a second attempt in summer 2004, most of the 165 workers signed union cards, and the store got union certification from the Labor Board in Montreal. You could just hear the gnashing of teeth in Bentonville. UFCW Local 1518 president Brooke Sundin pointed out that "Wal-Mart really doesn't have a choice. Under Quebec labor law, if the company doesn't negotiate, a provincial mediator can be appointed to assist the parties in reaching an agreement."

Sure enough, in October Wal-Mart showed its true colors, with its typical threat when a union's at the door. Spokesman Andrew Pelletier said, "If we are not able to reach a collective agreement that is reasonable and that allows the store to function efficiently and ultimately [be] profitable, it is possible that the store will close." Sure enough, Wal-Mart closed it.

In Saskatchewan, it's been move and counter-move in the union battle at the Weyburn Wal-Mart. After a majority of eligible workers signed union membership cards, the provincial Labour Relations Board (SLRB) held hearings. A Wal-Mart manager giving testimony let it slip out that the company gives all its managers a little document called "Wal-Mart: A Manager's Toolbox to Remaining Union Free" (see sidebar).

Bombshell! The Board subpoenaed the retailer for its

The Trusty Toolbox

Bentonville may not provide its store managers with the budget for adequate staffing, but it makes darn sure that every manager has the "Manager's Toolbox to Remaining Union Free." This confidential document cautions them to be ever vigilant for the tell-tale signs of union activity, such as "frequent meetings at associates' homes" or "associates who are never seen together . . . talking or associating with each other." Should they spot any such activity, they're instructed to call a special hotline to Bentonville. A corporate jet will soon be on its way, delivering a crack union-busting team to the threatened store. This team subjects all employees to days of mandatory anti-union indoctrinations—reinforcing the one they got in their new-hire orientation.

"toolbox." But did Wal-Mart hand it over? Not a chance. It turned to the Saskatchewan Court of Queen's Bench, challenging the authority of the SLRB to even rule in the matter.

That court ruled in Wal-Mart's favor. But the workers filed their own appeal. In the next higher court, a three-person panel ruled unanimously to overturn the Queen's Bench decision and to reinstate the subpoena. The panel directed Wal-Mart to provide the requested information to the SLRB, which would then determine its relevancy as evidence.

Wal-Mart is considering whether to take this to the Supreme Court of Canada. Once again: stay tuned, folks.

And China? In November 2004, Wal-Mart choked back all its anti-union instincts and said it would welcome the powerful, 123-million-members-strong Communist Party All

Leaving So Soon? I Wouldn't Hear of It!

The lawsuits against Wal-Mart by workers forced to work without meal breaks or rest breaks, or to put in overtime hours "off the clock," just keep piling up. When these suits are filed by individuals or a single store's workforce, Wal-Mart generally flicks them away like so much lint on its sleeve. But when one gains certification as a class-action suit—either statewide or nationwide—Wal-Mart snaps to attention.

With similar suits filed in thirty-nine states, it's hard to keep up with all of them. But one of the biggest, filed in 2001 and certified as a statewide class action in October 2004, includes all current and former "associates" who had worked in Washington state Wal-Mart stores since 1995 and did not advance to the management level—a potential class of forty thousand workers.

The plaintiffs' press release states that "Wal-Mart has a strict No Overtime policy which it enforces by disciplining

China Federation of Trade Unions (ACFTU) into its Chinese stores *if* the "associates" there requested it. When the ACFTU threatened to sue Wal-Mart and other foreign companies for their noncompliance, Bentonville blinked.

ALWAYS AN APPEAL:
STILL NO JUSTICE FOR WAL-MART PHARMACISTS

Our second edition offered the tale of a lawsuit by over one thousand current and former Wal-Mart pharmacists. In August 1999, we related, a Denver judge ruled that Wal-Mart had long violated labor laws by not paying overtime and had to pay back wages.

employees who work more than 40 hours per week without prior authorization. Understaffing of the stores, however, leaves employees with too much work to complete in 40 hours."

The original plaintiff, Georgie Hartwig, said that every week she had to work two to five hours over her "clocked in" time, and she saw even her recorded hours "disappear" when Wal-Mart manipulated her time records. Her attorney, Beth Terrell of the law firm Tousley Brain Stephens, blamed the retailer's "bottom-line culture that encourages managers to treat their workers illegally. Wal-Mart's managers have financial incentives to suppress store expenses—and they do so on the backs of their hourly workers."

Local Seattle ABC news affiliate KOMO asked Wal-Mart shoppers for their reactions. Said customer Rick Driver of Lynwood, "If this is true then I don't think I would shop here anymore. If that's the way they treat their people, that's not right."

We pointed out the industry standard: Our favorite pharmacy, owned by a Fort Worth-Dallas family-owned firm, pays pharmacists strictly by the hour—and time-and-a-half for overtime. And the half-dozen or more pharmacists we've known the past couple of decades, all employed by reputable organizations, have had comparable relations with their employers.

Wal-Mart is, so far as we know, the only major discounter that takes exception to the pay-by-the-hour rule. The Arkansas discounter argues that its pharmacists are salaried employees, not hourly workers, and should not get overtime pay or compensation for working over forty hours. The

Denver judge thought otherwise, saying in its summary judgment that Wal-Mart treated its pharmacists as hourly workers by telling them to go home when business was slow and docking their pay accordingly. The pharmacists also argued that they worked many hours off the clock doing paperwork and filing insurance claims for customers . . . often working sixty hours a week instead of their scheduled forty hours.

Each pharmacist was owed $50,000 to $75,000, according to Gerald Bader, a lawyer with a second law firm representing the pharmacists—a total of over $100 million in back pay, including interest. And that figure didn't include other damages: the court could have ordered Wal-Mart to pay missed wages for an additional year if it found that the discounter intentionally short-changed its employees.

Fast-forward all the way to 2004, and—you guessed it—we find Wal-Mart requesting a new hearing because, it claimed, the judge hadn't heard all the evidence! Five years later and still no justice for the pharmacists. And certainly still no payment for all those extra hours they toiled.

We Get Letters . . .

THIS UNION IS SERIOUS

We were delighted to get this letter from Randy Korgan, a member of the Teamsters Union in Southern California.

> I just picked up a copy of your book *How Wal-Mart Is Destroying the World*, and I am reading it. What struck me immediately was the preface that read, "Will this union—and others—mount a serious nationwide campaign while there's still a chance?"
>
> I am the Organizing Director of Teamsters Local 63 in Southern California and Chairman of the Wal-Mart Organizing Project for Southern California.

At this point we have gathered a tremendous amount of information and research and need to gather much more, because as your book says, "It is bigger than David versus Goliath." You obviously deeply despise Wal-Mart as we do. Any organization that destroys workers' lives and communities as Wal-Mart does cannot go unnoticed by anybody who has a passion for equality.

I look forward to possibly talking with you or meeting with you.

. . . And We Get Calls

We were alerted to the plight of a widow whose grown son, her only child, was mentally challenged. He had worked at Wal-Mart for several years in a job suited for his limited abilities, and he was well-liked there. But on one occasion he stayed in the restroom for too long—perhaps half an hour. His immediate boss went to the assistant manager, who promptly fired the young man. The mother was devastated.

We've heard from several new hires at Wal-Mart that employees are under the constant stare of department managers, assistant department managers, security guards, assistant store managers, and the all-seeing electric eye focused on every aisle—and particularly the camera focused on the employees' restrooms. Some said they simply couldn't stand the pressure of *always* being watched. *Always!* Just one more reason why Wal-Mart is reputed to have the highest turnover of any discounter in the history of American business.

GREEDY WAY #2: Suppliers Are Squeezed

Wal-Mart has a lot of clout: a nice fat order from this mega-retailer would seem to be the dream of many manufacturers. Wrong, wrong, wrong!

Because Wal-Mart is so big, it can (and does!) demand just about anything it wants from its vendors, from deeper-than-usual discounts to downright disadvantageous shipping policies to enforced returns on slow-moving merchandise. Some manufacturers are getting to the point where they just say "No" to doing business with Wal-Mart: the huge sale is not worth the even huger headache.

In December 2003, *Fast Company* magazine ran a beaut of a cover story: "The Wal-Mart You Don't Know." It uncovered the ugly truth about the iron fist of Bentonville and its crushing effect on U.S. suppliers. Reporter Charles Fishman had his work cut out for him: nobody who currently does business with the mega-retailer would talk to him about it.

So Fishman had to track down folks who *used* to work for or advise a Wal-Mart supplier. A consultant he talked to explained it this way: "You won't hear anything negative from most people. It would be suicide. If Wal-Mart takes something the wrong way, it's like Saddam Hussein. You just don't want to piss them off."

One former beverage supplier told Fishman, "Everyone from the forklift driver on up to me, the CEO, knew we had to deliver [to Wal-Mart] on time. Not ten minutes late. And not forty-five minutes early. . . . You have this thirty-second delivery window. Either you're there, or you're out."

But even as suppliers struggle to dance to Wal-Mart's tune, they are pushed to deliver the same goods for less each year, until their profits dwindle to nothing. As *Fast Company* describes it, Wal-Mart's disingenuous goal is simply to offer its customers the lowest possible prices. "But what almost no one outside the world of Wal-Mart and its twenty-one thousand suppliers knows is the high cost of those low prices. . . . To survive in the face of its pricing demands, makers of everything from bras to bicycles to blue jeans have had to lay off employees and close U.S. plants in favor of outsourcing products from overseas."

So why don't suppliers just say "No" to Wal-Mart and take their business elsewhere? Well, for retail suppliers of any size, that's no longer an option. Wal-Mart is just too dominant. *Fast Company* quoted Gib Carey, a partner at the global business consulting firm Bain & Co.: "Wal-Mart is the essential retailer, in a way no other retailer is. Our clients cannot grow without finding a way to be successful with Wal-Mart."

Here are some of the other things Wal-Mart does to its vendors—so often that these practices begin to feel like unwritten policies.

CLAIM SHIPMENT DAMAGE WHENEVER YOU CAN

Remember my interview with Joe, the former Wal-Mart manager who finally quit after over fifteen years? He told me how he had one "complaint" employee whose main job it was to claim product damage, or to tell vendors that the product was not received or that the pallets it came on were damaged. And when Wal-Mart claimed damage (which was often), vendors had to take Wal-Mart's word on it—or lose a huge customer. Quite by accident, we once overheard a conversation that seemed to imply that Wal-Mart's damage policies are fishy indeed. Two food brokers from different companies had sold to the mega-retailer; and both were evaluating whether they were actually losing money by doing so. The reason? Wal-Mart's tendency to deduct alleged damage on shipments. They are "worse than all the others put together," said one of the brokers.

DEMAND MORE AND MORE FROM VENDORS

The *Los Angeles Times* noted that, contrary to the standard practice of most big retailers, some truckers are expected to

Could Wal-Mart Be Too Cheap Even for China?

When the world's largest maker of microwave ovens complains about Wal-Mart—and they're in China, Wal-Mart's main source for ultra-cheap goods that allow them high, high markups—we're more than happy to pass the word along.

David Shen is marketing director for Guangdong Galanz Enterprise, which will ship 14 million ovens in 2004. Of these, 700,000 will end up on Wal-Mart shelves under other brand names. Shen says Wal-Mart demands such a low price, his company makes no profit on them. "Wal-Mart is only price, price, price," he complains.

Before Wal-Mart's Chinese suppliers signed on, they should have talked to a representative group of U.S. manufacturers who have had to close shop because of Wal-Mart's demands for cheaper and cheaper wholesale prices.

unload the cargo themselves when they arrive at Wal-Mart. Oh, Wal-Mart staff will do it—IF the shipper pays them. Independent driver George Hauschild of Palm Springs is quoted: "They're awful. They don't even let you use the bathroom."

Fortune magazine notes that late in 2003 Wal-Mart issued a new demand to suppliers: label every single box and pallet shipped to the retailer with a radio frequency identification (RFID) tag, the better to help Wal-Mart keep inventories lean and mean and reduce "shrinkage." It's yet another extra cost and hassle for suppliers already squeezed nearly dry by Wal-Mart's demands. No RFID tags? Sorry, no sales to Wal-Mart.

Fortune said some retail analysts estimate Wal-Mart could *save* over $8 billion a year with RFID; others estimate that it will *cost* each of Wal-Mart's suppliers $13 million to $23 million up front to put the system in place—a hole they'll have to climb out of before reaping any of their own savings from the technology.

SELL U.S. WORKERS DOWN THE RIVER

A November 2003 article in the *Los Angeles Times* describes the "Vendors Alley" at Wal-Mart headquarters where sales reps meet with Wal-Mart buyers. The article quoted Chicago manufacturer Carl Krauss: "Your price is going to be whittled down like you never thought possible." Like so many other U.S. manufacturers under relentless cost-cutting pressure from Wal-Mart, Krauss has been forced to move operations to China: 40 percent of his goods are now made there by workers earning twenty-five cents an hour. Asked about making that wrenching choice, Krauss admits, "My father was dead set against it. I have the same respect for American workers, but I'm going to do what I have to do to survive."

Following the 2004 PBS broadcast of *Frontline*, "Is Wal-Mart Good for America?" correspondent/producer Hedrick Smith joined a live online discussion on the *Washington Post* website. One viewer wrote in, "It was obvious that getting an employer to talk openly about the pressure on them to relocate their operations to China was difficult." Smith replied, "Some said privately that Wal-Mart has told them point blank that they must move production overseas. . . . Some say that Wal-Mart buyers even check up on them to see if they are meeting what amounts to a quota to overseas production that

Wal-Mart has given them—something close to 30 percent—especially if they want to sell to Wal-Mart's low 'opening price' point marketing program." He noted, though, that none of these vendors was willing to say these truths on camera.

Here, from *Fast Company* magazine's December 2003 cover story, "The Wal-Mart You Don't Know," are a few examples of U.S. jobs lost to satisfy the Bentonvillains' demands for ever cheaper products:

- ✪ Carolina Mills of North Carolina supplies raw materials to apparel makers who sell half of their goods to Wal-Mart. The company did well until 2000; since then, as those apparel makers have either gone overseas or shut down, Mills has closed ten of its original seventeen factories and given pink slips to fourteen hundred employees.

- ✪ Levi Strauss once had sixty U.S. manufacturing plants. It moved 25 percent of operations overseas between 1981 and 1990—before Wal-Mart began flexing real muscle—but two U.S. factories remained, employing over twenty-five hundred workers. In 2003, Levi cut a deal with Wal-Mart to provide the retailer with a new, cheaper "Signature" line of jeans. By offering quantity, not quality, Levi saw its sales and profits rebound. It immediately closed its last two U.S. factories and laid off all its garment workers there—21 percent of its workforce.

Where will it end? Steve Dobbins of Carolina Mills gets it about right: "People ask, 'How can it be bad for things to come into the U.S. cheaply? How can it be bad to have a bargain at Wal-Mart?' Sure, it's held inflation down, and it's great to have bargains. But you can't buy anything if you're not employed. We are shopping ourselves out of jobs."

CANCEL ORDERS IMMEDIATELY WHEN BUSINESS SLOWS

Vendors tell me that when sales reports tell the headquarters in Bentonville that sales are weak, Wal-Mart is notorious for canceling orders or refusing shipment on orders right away. This disregard for manufacturers is the sort of thing that can send smaller or less-prepared suppliers into serious trouble—even bankruptcy—on Wal-Mart's whim.

RENEGE ON VENDOR CONTRACTS

We read the sad tale of the Lovable Company, once the country's sixth-largest maker of intimate apparel. Wal-Mart became Lovable's biggest customer—then turned on them. "They had awarded us a contract, and . . . they changed the terms so dramatically that they really reneged," said former president Frank Garson. Less than three years later, the seventy-two-year-old company closed its doors. Reporter Charles Fishman found Garson hesitant to say too much for fear of litigation, but he did share this final opinion of the mega-retailer: "They leave a lot to be desired in the way they treat people. Their actions to pulverize people are unnecessary. Wal-Mart chewed us up and spit us out."

FORCE DISCOUNTS ON SUPPLIERS

As you may know, many suppliers offer a 2-percent discount if bills are paid within ten days of invoicing. According to *Forbes* magazine, Wal-Mart usually pays its bills closer to thirty days—but routinely takes a 2-percent discount even then. What's more, Wal-Mart takes the discount on the gross amount of the invoice rather than the net amount, which deducts for costs like shipping—larger amount, larger discount, and bad, bad manners from a company with the clout to throw its weight around like this.

USE A LITTLE SUBTLE INTIMIDATION

We still love that story of an executive's first visit to the buying offices of Sam's Club. There, among the unfinished plywood walls and folding tables and chairs, were signs greeting visitors that read: "How Low Can You Go?" Well, at least you know where you stand going into the interrogation, er, negotiation.

We Get Letters . . .

Bud Dell of Waterloo, Iowa, sent us these two tales of construction contractors who've sworn never to do business with Wal-Mart again:

> A few years ago I was talking to a fellow who had a pickup with a large flatbed. He and his crew spray-painted the Kmarts in a five-state area. I asked him about the new Wal-Mart they were building in the area. He said he would not contract with them. He had painted a store in Fort Dodge, Iowa, and [Wal-Mart] would not pay him for the job. He ended up getting fifty cents on the dollar.
>
> Today at a local coffee shop a cement contractor was telling us how Wal-Mart beat him out of a good number of dollars on a parking lot. He got the contract for the lot, and as he was working on the site they kept making changes. He billed them for the additional work and they wouldn't pay, saying the work was not authorized by their headquarters. He said he never did get all his money, and this is an ongoing thing with small subcontractors.

Nancy Ludwig of Johnstown, Pennsylvania, writes:

> I want to thank you for writing your book. I was beginning to think something was wrong with me, because I'm the only one in my family who hates Wal-Mart.

I work driving city buses in Johnstown, belong to a union, and am a coal miner's daughter who believes in buying American-made products, only it's getting harder every day to find them. Wal-Mart advertised "Bring it home" [but] you're lucky to find writing paper in that store that's made in the U.S.A. . . .

My brother works for a factory that makes a chemical in underarm deodorant. Rumor has it that Wal-Mart reps came and told them they wanted a 5 percent reduction in what they paid last year for their products or they wouldn't sell them. I told my brother to buy your book.

FOUR REASONS TO BEWARE OF WAL-MART

It's no secret that we hate Wal-Mart. Those Bentonvillains have been under this author's skin for more than twenty-one years now, and we don't love those blankety-blanks any more now than we ever have—which is not at all. Want to know another of the many things we hate about Wal-Mart? You can't trust it any more than you could trust Satan with a snow cone. Here's why.

REASON #1: Promises, Promises

Once upon a time, when Wal-Mart had just a handful of stores, Sam Walton called a managers' meeting. The wife of one manager, fearing that the chain would one day open seven days a week, was assured by Sam himself that two things were certain (no, not those two things):

✪ The chain would never, ever, ever open on a Sunday.

✪ The chain would never, ever, triple never sell alcohol, in any form.

(Remember, Sam's other never, ever rule—that he'd never, ever go into a town where Wal-Mart is not wanted? If you wonder what became of that rule, you might want to go back and look at chapter 2.)

What can Sam have been meaning, to make promises like this, that he was never going to keep? Look what happened:

Retailers in the small town of Pella, Iowa, had always observed Sunday as a day of rest. The first nine years that Wal-Mart was in town, it seemed to respect this taboo. Then suddenly, around 1990, orders came from headquarters in Bentonville: the store must open between twelve and five on Sunday. So much for the corporation's promise—and so much for sensitivity to local feelings.

But it gets worse.

Wal-Mart, by its own policy, is now universally open on Sunday, unless prohibited by a state or local law. This pretty much forces the competition to open on Sunday, too, if they want to stick around. What is more, Wal-Mart employees with strong religious beliefs have been forced into an impossible dilemma: work on their Sabbath or lose their job.

According to the *Wall Street Journal*, Scott Hamby worked at Wal-Mart in Bolivar, Missouri, until he was fired for refusing to work on Sunday, preferring to go to church. According to Hamby, his manager's reaction to his situation was to tell the woman in charge of setting staff schedules to "keep Scott here on Sunday until he quits." Hamby, a devout Christian and a graduate of Southwest Bible College, needed his job but cherished his convictions still more. He felt he had no recourse but to sue. A court in Springfield, Missouri, sided with Hamby.

In the wake of this lawsuit, Wal-Mart was forced to change its policies to accommodate those who prefer to worship someone other than Sam on Sunday. The *Wall Street Journal* also notes that this settlement "could have far-reaching implications for other companies with weekend staffing needs that conflict with workers' religious practices."

Guess Sam met his match this time.

But what about liquor?

Oh, yes. Well, since Sam made "never, ever" promise number two ("Wal-Mart will never, ever sell alcohol, in any form"), Wal-Mart has become, by most estimates, the biggest nationwide purveyor of beer and wine.

So, two solemn pledges, two utterly broken promises. We do wish those other "dependables" (death and taxes, that is) were this easy to get around, don't you?

REASON #2: Always the Low Road

Wal-Mart got by with the slogan "Always the Lowest Price. Always" for years, until the National Advertising Review Board, which is funded by the Better Business Bureau, investigated the claim that Wal-Mart always has the low(est) price. The Board found that this just was not and is not true, and promptly ordered our pals in Bentonville to stop saying it.

Wal-Mart then had to change its motto to something that barely skipped around the law—like "Always Low Prices. Always"—so near their original slogan that the public in general still perceived that Wal-Mart had the lowest prices.

Bob Moore, publisher of the *Star-Progress* in Berryville, Arkansas (the Waltons' home turf), asked his editor and columnist, Tom Larimer, to launch an investigation. He felt free from Wal-Mart's wrath, inasmuch as the Bentonville discounter had already withdrawn advertising support from the small-town newspapers to which, in large part, the Walton family owed its earliest success in Arkansas.

Larimer described the "shopping tour" in his column, "Potpourri." Staffers came up with a list of nineteen items— from ballpoint pens to peanut butter. They divided the list in half and chose shopping days that were separated by at least

Always High Prescription Prices?

Don't believe all that hot air about Wal-Mart having the lowest price . . .on anything.

Take prescriptions. That's one department in which older customers might believe they can save money. But remember, Wal-Mart's "always the lowest price" is rarely, we'd guess, a reality.

We got local proof when we ran into Allan Carmena at our favorite pharmacy, Minyard's—family-owned, founded by a Dallas/Fort Worth family over fifty years ago. Mr. Carmena thought that Minyard's prices were a little too high, so he shopped "all over town" for a better deal.

Happily, he came back to Minyard's—and before getting his prescription filled, he asked with a grin: "Who do you think has the highest prescription prices in Fort Worth?"

We ventured a guess: "Wal-Mart."

Bingo!

Carmena showed the Minyard pharmacist his findings for the prescriptions that (we assumed) he and his wife take on a quarterly basis.

Wal-Mart:	$464.46
AARP mail order:	$443.10
Minyard's:	$415.76

How we'd love to post this sign in front of every Wal-Mart store in the country:

"Wal-Mart. We Make You *Think* We've Got Low Prices. Always!"

Watch Out for That Opening Price Point

On *Frontline*, former Wal-Mart manager Jon Lehman walked us through one of the key ways Wal-Mart hooks its customers: the "opening price points." These are the un-believably cheap items you can't miss when you walk into the Supercenter, prominently displayed in stand-alone towers or stacked at the end of each aisle. Your immedi-ate impression: "Wow, what great low prices!" Dazzled by all these bargains, you venture down the aisles. And even though the goods you'll find there sell for ordinary prices—in fact, possibly more than they sell for at a com-peting retailer's—you're lulled into spending whatever Wal-Mart charges for the items you really came for.

Customers do buy the opening price points, of course; Lehman says it's often a "feeding frenzy" and the item will sell out in a day. But with Wal-Mart's lightning-fast inven-tory response, managers can order more until the ware-house runs out.

The goal, of course, is the profit to be made not on the opening price points, but on the everyday items that cus-tomers go on to buy. It's a little more subtle than "bait and switch," because customers end up doing the switching for themselves.

two weeks to avoid skewing the results with specials they might have encountered on only one shopping day. They picked six nearby stores—including Wal-Mart, of course—and set off to fill their shopping bags.

In the final analysis, Wal-Mart was cheapest on only two items—this on the first shopping day.

On the second day, Wal-Mart was the most expensive place to shop—and the investigators had the register tapes to prove it.

Surveys like this one soon became a favorite newspaper activity. After members of the Arkansas Press Association (APA) met with Wal-Mart VP of marketing, Paul Higham—and got a long-winded brush-off—they did their own informal survey.

They learned that—surprise!—prices for the same products are not the same at every Wal-Mart outlet, according to an Arkansas Press Association newsletter. If there is a Target or Kmart store nearby, that Wal-Mart's prices are forced lower. "The bottom line: the Wal-Mart customer in a smaller community is paying more than the customer in the next town where there's a Kmart or Target."

At least one other survey—conducted by a Texas Press Association staff member in the Austin area—found Kmart's prices lower, on average, than Wal-Mart's or Target's for goods ranging from garden hoses to Barbie dolls.

We hope all this will motivate you to do a little price comparison on the items you purchase regularly.

REASON #3: Untruth in Advertising

Michigan's attorney general brought suit against Wal-Mart for alleged violations in the state's consumer protection act. According to the *Wall Street Journal*, Michigan's attorney gen-

The Bottom Line

As Wal-Mart chews its way into new territory, spitting out regional grocery chains as it advances, all those starry-eyed new Wal-Mart grocery shoppers should pay heed to a survey published by the Rochester, New York *Democrat and Chronicle* in June 2004. This regular feature checks the prices on fifteen common food items at two supermarket chains and at Wal-Mart Supercenters. The previous nine surveys had produced a tie for lowest prices between Wal-Mart and Wegmans Food Market. This time, Tops Friendly Market edged them both out. Wal-Mart charged more for fresh chicken breasts (from $1.44 to $2.34 more per pound) and eggs, and for popular brands of toothpaste, spaghetti sauce, crackers, laundry detergent, orange juice, and candy. The startling bottom line: on the checkout total, both supermarkets beat Wal-Mart by 5 or 6 percent.

The lesson for you: Don't abandon your long-time supermarket just because the big new bully on the block puts a "loss leader" at the end of every aisle. Do some comparison shopping.

Another thought: Unless you're really strapped, don't base your store choice only on price. Think about whether spending an extra dollar or few each week might mean you're shopping with clerks and shelf-stockers who have a little financial breathing room themselves. Maybe even decent health insurance, too.

eral discovered that Wal-Mart's in-store advertisements were misleading: they "compared products that were not the same size or model without noting the difference, and . . . the ads sometimes inflated the prices competitors charged." Wal-Mart settled, agreeing to various changes in the way it compares its prices to those of competitors. Hey, how about honestly and accurately, for starters?

It also may interest you to know that it is "against store policy" to allow customers to jot down prices in a Wal-Mart. That's what Virginia Berger of Spring Hill, Florida, was told when she was accosted in a Wal-Mart doing just that, according to an AP wire story. Mrs. Berger, who lives with her husband on pension and disability benefits, says she was "angry and embarrassed, and I thought they were going to throw me out." She later found no problem in writing down prices at Kmart or Target. What is the meaning of this, we wonder?

REASON #4: The China Syndrome

We can still remember it. Can you?

Wal-Mart's old red-white-and-blue marketing campaign, "Buy American." We haven't seen much of it since Sam Walton passed on. Now Wal-Mart sources an enormous amount of its merchandise from China—$15 billion worth in 2003. The retailer accounts for fully 10 percent of all U.S. imports from China. On *Frontline*'s "Is Wal-Mart Good for America?" former store manager Jon Lehman described the dramatic change that took place about a year or two after Sam Walton died.

Wal-Mart hit a rough patch financially, and the Benton-villains discovered the nice, fat profit that can be made from imports. They were used to making 18 or 20 percent on U.S.-

CHINA ... CHINA ... BANGLADESH ... KOREA
WHERE'S THE STUFF THAT'S MADE IN
AMERICA?

made goods. But on products from China, Macao, Bangladesh, says Lehman, they could make 60, 70, 80 percent. What a shot in the arm for the ol' profit-and-loss statement! And there was no question of passing any of that lucre along to store employees in the form of, oh, maybe a living wage. Those profits were earmarked for the almighty shareholders, right up to and including the Walton family treasury. "Buy American" was history. And Wal-Mart's long-suffering American suppliers found out just how much tougher and meaner the retailer could be when it had a dirt-cheap source for goods.

Lehman described the desperate measures taken at Wal-Mart after *Dateline* exposed all the imports the stores were selling under the "Made in USA" banner:

> We had to go through all of our stores and pull every "Buy America" sign, every "Made in the USA" sign, everything that was red, white and blue that was hanging on the walls. We even had permanent signs that were liquid-nailed to the cement walls, concrete walls, that we had to rip down that said "Buy America." And it had to be done by a certain deadline. And if you didn't do it, your job was on the line. It was an emergency situation.

Now the official line from Bentonville is that Wal-Mart's been *forced* to buy from China. Lehman recalls a recent speech by Lee Scott, in which the CEO was asked why the company did so much business in China. His response? "This is a global economy now. We've got to do business with China. We have no other choice."

Don't you believe it. Wal-Mart led the way.

Come One, Come All

Many international observers and human rights advocates were horrified when China—whose hearty embrace of capitalism seems to have increased, rather than curbed, its truly shameful labor practices—was granted membership in the World Trade Organization (WTO) in 2001. But big retailers cheered, of course, because in return for letting China join their club, they got the deal from China that they'd all been waiting for: over a period of years, stiff tariffs would be lowered, trade barriers lifted, and access to all those upwardly mobile Chinese consumers would at last be granted. And starting on December 11, 2004, the third anniversary of China's WTO membership, overseas companies were allowed to set up as many of their own shops in China as they want.

Wal-Mart's slice of the pie? Well, the retailer already does more trade with China than does either Russia or the United Kingdom. In fact, 80 percent of Wal-Mart's imports are from China—$15 billion worth in 2003, and *China Business Weekly* projected a 20 percent increase to $18 billion in 2004. (We might just point out here that the United States' trade deficit with China may top *$150 billion* for 2004.) If anyone should get the red carpet in China, it's the buddies from Bentonville. Indeed, Wal-Mart already had 40 stores (albeit not wholly owned, but with local partners) in major Chinese cities, and it plans to add fifteen more in 2005. And those will all still be with Chinese partners, says CEO Lee Scott.

Royko Weighs In

You think I get nasty with Wal-Mart? The late Mike Royko, the nationally syndicated columnist, really dealt that crummy discounter a haymaker in his column:

Eric Mattys of St. Charles, Illinois, bought some tires for his pickup from a Sam's Club store. He was told to come back in forty-five minutes. When he came back, the man who had put the tires on was gone—and so was the truck. The man was traced and found the next day with the truck—which was stripped. He had sold the mirrors, toolbox, stereo—everything that could be sold. The pickup wouldn't run, and Eric had to pay $220 to get the shell of the thing towed home.

Back to the store he went. A manager gave him a claim number. It turns out that Wal-Mart stores are self-insured. So Eric called Bentonville. The man he talked to tried to intimidate Eric, saying the truck had been stolen by an individual and he "couldn't believe I [Eric] was trying to make a claim against Wal-Mart."

Mike ended his column with nothing but contempt for the multibillionaire members of the Walton family. "The interest income a single Walton would earn while going to the bathroom at 3 AM would be enough to buy Eric a good used truck. People can be so greedy. God bless Wal-Mart," Mike concluded.

We Get Letters . . .

SCHOOL REFORM, WAL-MART STYLE

Dianne Engelsen of Arlington, Washington, wrote to inform us that Wal-Mart is funneling some of the profits made on the backs of its workers into an anti-union organization:

> I just finished your book in one sitting. Well done! You confirm a lot of things I suspected and validate my vow never to set foot in a Wal-Mart store.
>
> One thing I didn't see mentioned in your book, however, is the Walton family's financial support of union-busting organizations like the Evergreen Freedom Foundation (EFF) here in Washington state.
>
> I'm a teacher at Marysville-Pilchuck High School in Marysville, a town with a very wealthy Native American tribe (the Tulalips). They just opened a huge casino next door to the Wal-Mart, which is built on tribal land. I understand there are issues regarding reduced school funding due to the fact that the store is on Tulalip land. Now Wal-Mart has announced its plans to make this site a Supercenter and the local grocers are shaking in their boots. Lots of reasons to hate Wal-Mart.
>
> But here's my biggest concern: I was recently involved in the longest school strike in state history. After thirty-six school days on strike, Marysville teachers were ordered back to work by a judge who commanded the district to pay us last year's wages. Actually, that was a relief, because the school board we were dealing with had not negotiated or compromised at all in seven weeks, and their last proposal still represented a cut in pay and four extra days of work without pay. What led the school board to its obstinate, hateful stance toward teachers? One of the school board members belongs to the EFF [Evergreen Freedom Foundation], a group that

bills itself as a "union watchdog" but that in fact encourages union busting. Check out this website to see what they're all about and to confirm the Walton Family Foundation's involvement: www.mediatransparency.org/recipients/eff.htm. . . .

We were ordered back to work by a court injunction, which we honored since we knew the school board had no intention of bargaining. Since then, three members of the school board have been voted out (and a recall petition has been submitted on the other two), despite the fact that the EFF allegedly contributed to the campaigns of each of the incumbents. Obviously, the public did not agree with what these people were trying to do to their teachers. . . .

Why does the Walton family want to break our teachers' union? Because they're evil, that's why. It's just one more way that Wal-Mart is destroying America. Hopefully, you can expose this aspect of their power (and abuse of power) in your next book.

We checked the Media Transparency website she mentioned, and we learned that the Walton Family Foundation gave EFF $300,000 from 1998 through 2000. Sam's son John runs the Foundation; *Fortune* magazine calls him an "educational activist" and the family's "social reformer." John's a big supporter of the push to privatize U.S. education at the expense of our public school system; he uses foundation money to support advocacy and legislation for school vouchers and tuition tax credits.

Your Wal-Mart dollars at work.

BE PREPARED!

Brian Gliem began his letter with "I have a great Wal-Mart story." And he's not foolin'! Here it is:

I manage a store for a family-owned grocery chain in

Sorry, Ma'am, But That Would Be Against Store Policy

That's the excuse a Wal-Mart "associate" gave to a seventy-three-year-old woman who was trapped by a newspaper vending machine in front of the store in Geneseo, Illinois. The newspaper in question—the *Moline Dispatch/ Rock Island Argus*—printed a detailed report of the whole sorry episode. It seems the woman had just bought a paper when the spring-loaded door snapped down onto the strings from her hood. She couldn't get them out, nor could she slip out of her jacket, and she had no more coins to use to open the door.

Finally, a young girl in a bright blue vest emerged from the store and asked if everything was all right. Seeing the woman's predicament, she went back into the store, then returned to tell the woman that the vending machines didn't belong to Wal-Mart and the store had a strict policy

Ohio. We pride ourselves on customer service, cleanliness, and, above all, honesty.

Wal-Mart opened a store in one of the small towns where we do business and then after about five years expanded to a Supercenter. One day, one of Wal-Mart's poorly trained, overworked employees, being new to the grocery business, put an entire pallet of eggs in the freezer instead of the cooler. Not wanting to be out of stock on one of the best-selling dairy items for the weekend, members of Wal-Mart's management took some money and started visiting the competition in hopes of buying enough eggs to get them through.

In this town we have two stores. They visited the

against "tampering" with them. But she offered to call the office of the newspaper and have them send someone out.

The trapped woman recalled, "I told her I just wanted someone to come and put some quarters in the thing and that's when she told me that they weren't responsible for making refunds for the machine."

The girl left again, then returned only to inform the woman that she hadn't been able to get anyone from the *Dispatch/Argus* on the phone.

"I told her that if she would just put some money in the machine, I would pay her back as soon as I could get some change," the woman said.

The trapped woman waited for nearly twenty minutes before the employee finally agreed to put two quarters in the machine and enable her escape.

(Thanks to Paul and Judy Wilcox of Penn Valley, California, for sharing this one. They "definitely plan to never set foot in a Wal-Mart again!")

first store and asked to see the manager. They represented themselves as Wal-Mart management and wanted to make a large purchase. Naturally our people declined the transaction, as the egg cartons had our name on them. The Wal-Mart people then visited the second store. Realizing that honesty wasn't going to get them anywhere, this time they represented themselves as leaders of a Boy Scout troop. They fabricated a story about needing lots of eggs for a breakfast and they had forgotten to order them.

Our company is very involved with the community, so our people bought this lie, hook, line, and sinker. We sold them as many eggs as we could spare, thinking we had just helped out some of the town's kids. Boy, were we wrong. Wal-Mart put our eggs on the shelf and sold them five cents cheaper, twisting the knife.

Word of this contemptible action spread quickly throughout the small community. The consequences not only involved the two rival stores, but also caused our community to be suspicious of anyone seeking merchandise or donations on behalf of the Boy Scouts. One of the leaders of a local Boy Scout troop wrote a letter of complaint to Wal-Mart and received no response or apology. Our guess: the Wal-Mart "associates" that pulled off this outrageous act were rewarded for their ingenuity.

5

SIX WAYS WAL-MART
IS DOWNRIGHT
BAD TO THE BONE

In December 2003, the DC-based United Church of Christ (UCC) issued the following call to action in their Justice and Peace Action Network (JPANet) weekly electronic alert:

Support Worker Justice: Send a Christmas Card to the Wal-Mart CEO

As the Christmas shopping season moves into high gear, we need to remember that too many items in our stores are produced or sold under conditions that are unfair, demeaning, or possibly harmful to workers. We can begin to transform the Christmas season from a time to buy into a time to advocate for justice and the fair treatment of all workers.

One way to act for justice is to participate in the UCC's 8th annual "Christmas Cards to CEOs" campaign. This year we are contacting the CEO of Wal-Mart to change the company's policies and practices that are unfair and inconsistent with the principles of good corporate social responsibility. . . .

In this season of Advent, send a Christmas card for

justice. Contact Wal-Mart CEO H. Lee Scott and urge Wal-Mart to improve its labor practices.

Our hat's off to them for a well-timed and well-targeted effort. It's heartening to hear of such organized opposition to the Bentonvillains among spiritual and social leaders.

Read through our description of six ways that Wal-Mart is bad through and through. Then, why not get out the phone book—or log onto the Internet—and find out which organizations are rallying to the cause in your neck of the woods? Bet they'd be delighted to have you help them fight the good fight.

WAY #1: Sweatshop Labor

In our last edition, we were still able to muster fresh outrage at Wal-Mart's low-profile abandonment of Mr. Sam's "Buy American" practices. Those days now seem long ago indeed. The push to produce retail goods cheaply overseas has proved irresistible. And no one has pushed harder than Wal-Mart.

Some would say there's nothing wrong with that: business is business. Consumers demand a good bargain, so what's a retailer to do? What's wrong, some would say, with paying only twenty-five cents of labor costs on a $19.95 pair of pants?

Well, several things. If you want a selfish reason, consider this: By the end of 2004, the United States' trade deficit was $580 billion and counting. Around the world, the value of our dollar is dwindling. Foreign investors are getting nervous. U.S. investors are starting to pull out of domestic stocks and shifting to international investments. Put this together with a federal budget deficit in the $400 billions and a national debt in the $700 billions, and you might say we happy consumers of cheap imports are all fiddling while Rome burns.

And if you want an unselfish reason, there's the toll of human misery on the foreign factory workers.

We got hold of Wal-Mart's *Factory Certification Report,* March 2003–February 2004 and couldn't put it down. Seriously, it's a page-turner. On the one hand, it's that classic voice of corporate Wal-Mart, putting its best face forward, first patting itself on the back for the improvements it's brought to humble villages in India and Bangladesh by using suppliers there and "vigilantly monitoring" working conditions, then earnestly describing said ongoing inspection procedures and the company's new supplier standards and compliance practices that went into effect January 2005.

On the other hand, the report reveals just how low those new standards are. For example:

> Work weeks exceeding 60 hours are unacceptable and considered a violation. Wal-Mart's maximum tolerance is a 72-hour work week over six days, or no more than 14 hours per calendar day. Factories should be working toward a maximum of 60 hours per work week.

You read that right, folks. No more than *14 hours a day, 72 hours a week.* That's the *new* standard. (And funny, isn't it, that twelve-hour difference between "unacceptable" and "maximum tolerance"?) Now just imagine the workdays (and nights) those workers must have put in *before* the new standards were enforced.

RED LIGHT, GREEN LIGHT

Wal-Mart applies a "traffic light system" to factory inspections. During the report's time period, only 20.69 percent (3,051 factories) received the top "Green" rating, 42.75 percent (6,306) were "Yellow," and 35.86 percent (5,290 factories) rated "Red."

A "Red" rating means the factory's guilty of at least one of these violations: not paying legally required benefits or overtime, not paying minimum wage, or paying wages without clear, verifiable records. "Yellow" violations include health and safety concerns, excessive working hours (sixty-one to seventy-two hours a week), and denying workers one day off a week. A "Green" rating doesn't mean the factory meets all standards; it could still have so-called low-risk violations, such as poor lighting, badly maintained restrooms, or inadequate cafeteria facilities—and these won't necessarily require corrective action.

There's one more category that's even worse than "Red." It takes a lot for a factory to earn a "Failed" rating—child labor, forced labor, attempted bribery of the inspector—but in the report year, 103 of the factories that supply Wal-Mart goods did get an F.

By the way, Wal-Mart defines "child labor" as work by children under age fourteen; after that age, apparently, they're considered fully capable of the "maximum tolerance" fourteen-hour days and seventy-two-hour weeks.

There's another big flaw to this certification system, of course, and it's a doozy. Most inspections are scheduled and announced well in advance, allowing plenty of time for managers to pretend to comply. Unannounced inspections come only after a complaint is filed by a worker. And human-rights activists have gathered evidence from sweatshop workers of the intimidation they feel from management—and the retribution they face if they complain or answer an inspector's questions too frankly.

Here's one example. In February 2004, the National Labor Committee and China Labor Watch reported that workers in a Chinese factory that makes plastic toys for Wal-Mart were being worked seven days a week, in shifts of up to *twenty and a half hours,* and were paid an average *16.5¢ an hour* (China's minimum wage was 31¢ an hour). Factory managers had "trained workers to answer prepared questions and paid

them a bonus for remembering them correctly during visits by Wal-Mart inspectors." During inspections at the factory in Chang Ping Township in Guangdong Province, managers would unlock fire exits and medical kits that were normally locked. Time cards were doctored to fake compliance.

That's bad enough. But the rights groups say the mega-retailer "appeared to condone the Chinese management's

Disposable Workers

Fifty-dollar boom boxes. Twenty-dollar CD players. How can Wal-Mart and other U.S. retailers obtain such dirt-cheap consumer electronics? The answer can be found in industrial Shenzhen, China, where poor villagers stream into a city filled with surplus workers and compete for factory jobs that pay pennies an hour. The machines are old. The workers have to reach inside to operate them. And each year, some forty thousand Chinese factory workers suffer a crushed or severed finger, hand, or arm.

One Shenzhen hospital now has a ward devoted to treating hand injuries. A Knight Ridder reporter interviewed one patient there, twenty-three-year-old Yan Kaiguo, who had lost the first joint of his index finger, crushed by a machine at a circuit-board plant.

Yan "feels lucky that he lost only part of his finger." He thinks once it's healed he'll still be able to work at his $96-a-month job. A hand surgeon at another hospital said "Every day, we get five or six cases like this, and sometimes over a dozen."

Shorter workdays, better pay, and safer equipment would raise prices. But then Wal-Mart's customers would have to pay more than twenty bucks for a CD player. That just wouldn't do, would it?

methods. No company could be that shallow or gullible, unless it were consciously acting out a role with the full intent of achieving the desired result—a whitewash." Wal-Mart countered with this gem: "It would be a complete violation of our policy for anyone to participate in any charade that would merely make a pretense of observing a thorough inspection." And we know Wal-Mart never, ever violates its own policies.

Says Andrew Tsuei, managing director of Wal-Mart's global procurement center in Shenzhen: "For the benefit of the consumer, we should buy merchandise where we get the best value."

But it's not only, or even mostly, the consumer who benefits. Whether Wal-Mart's hundreds of overseas agents—and their big bosses back in Bentonville—claim to know it or not, human beings on the other side of the globe are being exploited, injured, and tossed aside to make the Waltons one of the richest families on earth—if not THE richest. And by us, that stinks.

WAY #2: Cutting Costs with Illegal Workers

You might think, considering the miserable wages the Bentonvillains pay their "associates" and the billions piling up in the Walton family coffers, the company wouldn't have to resort to hiring undocumented workers—those who are in the United States illegally. Or then again, maybe you'd think that's just why they *would*.

So we weren't really shocked to read these headlines: "Immigration Officials Raid Wal-Mart." "Raid Rounds Up 300 Illegals At Wal-Mart." "Wal-Mart Cleaners Arrested In Raids." It happened in October 2003: Federal agents stormed into sixty-one stores in twenty-one states and arrested some 250 cleaning-crew workers. Even the inner sanctum of Bentonville headquarters was breached, and agents carried away cartons of documents from an executive's office. And you gotta love the feds for this: they called it "Operation Rollback."

Bentonville went into full damage control. Those aren't

our employees, they said. An agency hired them. They are subcontractors of subcontractors.

"We did not know," said that familiar Wal-Mart spokesperson, Mona Williams (she has been one busy mouthpiece lately). "Our understanding was that these third-party agencies had only legal workers." Of course, the retailer is "cooperating fully with investigators."

Did Wal-Mart know? That's the $64,000 question. If the feds can prove the retailer *knowingly* chose contractors who used undocumented workers, it could face hundreds or thousands in civil penalties per violation. If the government can prove Wal-Mart deliberately used contractors to avoid the trouble of confirming workers' legal status, the consequences could be far more serious. And what about the ten undocumented workers caught in the raid who turned out to be *on the Wal-Mart payroll?*

It's not as if Wal-Mart hadn't already had a wake-up call. The sweeping 2003 raids were a follow-up to two Pennsylvania investigations in 1998 and 2000. Those led to arrests of cleaning-crew workers at several Wal-Marts, $5 million in fines against the contractors, and sealed felony indictments.

In December 2003, Wal-Mart acknowledged that a federal grand jury panel had been convened in Pennsylvania to consider violations there. And the company issued an ingenious new defense: It had been "helping" the feds with their investigation for three years leading up to the twenty-one state raids. They had even delayed a planned transition to hiring their own cleaning crews, they claimed, so that the investigators would have plenty of time to gather evidence. Mona Williams said they had done so at the government's request. "We were simply stunned by the raids."

The plot keeps thickening. In June 2004, seventeen Mexican and Eastern European janitors—many of whom were among those arrested—filed a civil suit against the mega-retailer. They were soon joined by more than two hundred other former Wal-Mart contract janitors, many from Eastern Europe, who they say were also illegal immigrants. The group holds Wal-Mart responsible for conspiring to hire illegal immigrants, denying them benefits and overtime, and creating hazardous working conditions. Wal-Mart filed a motion to dismiss, saying the immigrants had no valid case.

Victor Zavala—father of the lead plaintiff, Victor Zavala, Jr.—says that the head of the agency that hired his family was tipped off by a Wal-Mart manager two months before the raids that a government investigation was under way. The agency then responded by adding a layer of protection: hiring subcontractors to manage and pay the illegal workers.

In August 2004, the *Wall Street Journal* and *The New York Times* reported that Wal-Mart was talking settlement with prosecutors in the federal investigation. When you hear that word *settlement*, you know Bentonville has weighed the bite of paying out settlement dollars (probably a couple million, in this case) against the bad PR of a court case that could expose some ugly truths about Ol' Smiley Face. When Wal-Mart settles, it gets to maintain its innocence.

This could be the smart choice, because some evidence has turned up that looks mighty bad for Bentonville:

✪ Back in 2002, Raymond Drude, the VP of Jani-King (one of the biggest U.S. cleaning companies), wrote a letter to Lee Scott. Jani-King had lost business in ten stores because a Wal-Mart district manager had given the contracts to illegal immigrants from Eastern Europe. He challenged the CEO to find out why Wal-Mart was "choosing non-taxpaying illegal aliens over local janitorial companies and their employees." (Wal-Mart officials claim they can't find this letter or any record that they received it.)

Not So Fast

In 2000, the Waltons' stockpile was worth approximately $100 billion. Seems that Wal-Mart stock wasn't immune to the general twenty-first century slump on Wall Street. And we're pleased to say the retailer has hit a few of its own bumps. In January 2004, CNN/Money observed "Wal-Mart Stores has grown so big so fast. But now it can't grow fast because it's so big." The number of stores keeps climbing, but not so each individual store's sales. One analyst opined that "poor recent results and management changes are leading to internal rethinking of [Wal-Mart's] aggressive deflationary pricing strategies . . ." For whatever reason, its stock value has been essentially flat since 2000.

❂ A professor of Russian language, Greta McCaughrin, says she wrote to then-CEO David Glass in 1999 to tell him immigrant janitors from Russia were being mistreated at a nearby Wal-Mart: "If Wal-Mart were a good neighbor to our community, it would not turn a blind eye to the plight of poor illegal immigrants. Your manager cannot be oblivious to the fact that they work in his store seven days a week, 364 days a year."

❂ In the cleaners' lawsuit, Teresa Jaros, a Polish immigrant who has cleaned Wal-Marts in three states, filed an affidavit that in 2003 a fellow cleaner had asked a Wal-Mart regional vice president to sponsor him for a green card.

Late in December 2004, a U.S. District Court judge denied Wal-Mart's motion to dismiss the immigrant janitors' lawsuit and approved the sending of court-approved notices to potential plaintiffs. Said Gilberto Garcia, a lawyer on the janitors' legal team: "The court found merit in the claim that illegal immigrant workers have minimum wage and overtime pay rights under the federal Fair Labor Standards Act. . . . This is a historic lawsuit, as far as immigration laws are concerned, as far as labor laws are concerned."

A lawyer for Wal-Mart said the judge's decision was "merely procedural."

WAY #3: Tax Hijinks

Fortune magazine's November 15, 2004 issue devoted thirteen pages to a profile of the Walton family: Sam's widow, Helen, and the four adult children. We learned that while frugal, frugal old Sam was still among us, he became so uncomfortable with the thought that Uncle Sam's estate taxes would take a chunk of his billions when he died that, like billionaires everywhere, he found a way around it. He set up his Wal-Mart stock holdings in a family partnership: 20 percent for each child, 10 percent each for himself and his wife. When he passed on in 1992, Helen inherited his share tax-free.

Now, the corporation pays a measly 0.8 percent dividend, but with each Walton holding tens of millions of shares, each collects almost $175 million a year for spending money. Surely, you'd think, the IRS and the Arkansas tax collector take a hefty bite from those earnings.

Think again.

Three of the Waltons now claim residency outside of Arkansas.

Daughter Alice's legal home is Texas, which has no state income tax.

Son John says Wyoming is his legal home ground. Again, no state income tax.

Easy Come, Easy Go

Remember those tax cuts the Bush administration tossed out into the sinking economy in Summer 2001? These dollars were not meant to be used by cash-strapped lower- and middle-class Americans to pay down credit-card debt or to sock away a little savings. No, they were meant to be transferred, as fast as lightning, into shopping-mall cash registers.

Now, like many companies in that sickening stock-market dive after the dot-com bubble burst, Wal-Mart had been watching its stock price slide—7.5 percent for the year.

But the Bentonvillains remembered the last tax rebate, back in 1975, that triggered a surge in consumer spending that goosed Wal-Mart's stock price up 157 percent, and they got to thinking about how they could get their hands on all those $300 and $600 checks arriving in American mailboxes. Why not provide a convenient service to their customers? One that would lure them into the stores with wads of greenbacks in hand?

The word went out: Come on down to any Wal-Mart, and the cheery "associates" will cash your rebate check—absolutely free of charge! And say! If you're in the mood for a shopping spree, why, no one's going to stop you. In fact—how may we help you?

Son Rob Walton's legal residence is Colorado. That state's single-bracket, flat-rate income tax (for 2004, 4.63 percent) is a boon for the wealthy.

Mother Helen and son Jim are the only Waltons still officially residing in Arkansas.

WAY #4: Pork-Barrel Treats

How's this for a great big glistening piece of pork? Al Norman's Sprawl-Busters website calls what went down in Lewiston, Maine, a "textbook case" of corporate welfare. In December 2001, after six months of secret negotiations with the mayor, other city officials, and even Maine's Governor Angus King, the public was given two days to digest the result: Wal-Mart's demands for a "level playing field" would cost the town and state close to *$20 million* in up-front and potential costs, including:

- ✪ $5.8 million in property tax reimbursements

- ✪ $1 million to relocate and expand sewer lines

- ✪ $940,000 for a new sand and gravel pit

- ✪ $800,000 for a new sand and gravel shed

- ✪ $300,600 worth of land (sixty-one acres)

- ✪ $45,000 for a commercial subdivision plan

- ✪ $18,300 in water and sewer fee reimbursements

and from the state's "business equipment tax reimbursement":

- ✪ A potential $7.8 million in personal property taxes

- ✪ $1.5 million for road relocations

- ✪ $180,000 for training

- ✪ Up to $348,750 in rebated state income tax from Wal-Mart's workers' payroll withholdings

And what did Lewiston get in return? A promise that Wal-Mart would hire 350 people to work thirty hours a week at $12 an hour—that's less than $19,000 a year. And as

Snakes Alive!

A good old boy in Pleasanton, Texas, reached for an automotive air filter in a Wal-Mart store and got a rattlesnake bite instead. I'll be damned if the Wal-Martians didn't claim he planted the snake there, but the fellow's attorney found that that particular Wal-Mart store had previously experienced snake problems from a nearby open field. Rather than settle this truly legitimate claim out of court, Snake Headquarters fought it in court. I'm pleased to say our hero finally received a $6,000 settlement.

Sprawl-Busters points out, the deal doesn't take into account all the jobs that will vanish as existing distribution networks get snuffed out.

Lewiston didn't have to line Wal-Mart's pockets for the privilege of having the monster muscle in. As Al Norman's site points out, in 1996 the town of Raymond, New Hampshire, had gotten a Wal-Mart distribution center more than twice the size of Lewiston's. Giveaways to Wal-Mart? Zip. In fact, says Raymond's town manager, "[Wal-Mart] offered us incentives."

WAY #5: Wal-Mart: "A Bad Neighbor"?

When you are a huge rich company and all you really want is to get huger and richer, it turns out that a lot of smaller, poorer people may have to get hurt in the process. Wal-Mart, with all its size and power, could hurt people or help them in a lot of situations. Which do you think it usually chooses to do?

County surveyor Jay Poe knows. "Wal-Mart is not a very

Sympathy for Their Nightmare

In our second edition, we shared the horror story of K. M. Fowler and his wife, who built a dream home for their golden years, only to have Wal-Mart move onto the property right behind them. That's when their dream became a nightmare. Wal-Mart's contractor took out a row of stately old oak trees. There was horrendous construction noise at all hours. Piles of trash blew from the parking lot into their neighborhood, and Wal-Mart customers wandered through. Wal-Mart brushed off all complaints, saying it bore no responsibility as it was only leasing the property.

Mr. Fowler's son created a website that tells the story in words and photos; you'll find it now at http://kimsey.stone pics.com/walmart.htm. Mr. Fowler has posted a few of the thousands of email messages he's gotten from others who have been ill-used by Wal-Mart. Most are sympathetic, and they make great reading. The few messages from *defenders* of Wal-Mart seem to rely, unfortunately, on viciousness and profanity, so viewer discretion is advised.

If Wal-Mart has set its sights on a property in your town, take Mr. Fowler's story to your city council, pronto.

good neighbor," he told the press when a drainage problem behind Huntington (Indiana) High School originating on Wal-Mart property next door was ignored by the discounter. The problem was caused when a Wal-Mart developer commissioned the store's landscaping. The landscaper terraced the planted green area incorrectly, and when it rained, the water seeped into the neighboring school's walls and severely damaged the tiles. "Fixing the [school's] tile is not our concern," concluded the developer. Schoolchildren's well-being is not important to Wal-Mart?

Wal-Mart secured thirty-eight acres to build a store in Central Kitsap, Washington. The site was right next to a tributary of Steel Creek, and heavy rains were due, according to local residents. Despite warnings, Wal-Mart, its developer, and its contractor decided to go right ahead with the earth moving to start construction.

Sure enough, the rains came, and the construction site's newly graded dirt and silt piled into the creek, wreaking untold damage on the ecosystem of salmon, other fish, and the eel-grass beds that fish depend on. According to environmental officials, it may be years before the habitat will recover from this senseless, easily preventable devastation.

While the state's Department of Ecology levied the largest fine in the state's history against Wal-Mart ($64,000), locals think it's still not enough. "We need to ask why the company took this risk. Perhaps it didn't matter to Wal-Mart," opined an editorial in the *Central Kitsap Reporter*. We think that writer has something there, don't you?

WAY #6: A Rotten Record with Women and Minorities

It's the biggest discrimination lawsuit in history. Originally filed by six female Wal-Mart workers, *Dukes v. Wal-Mart* was granted class-action status by a federal court in June 2004. That means it covers all women who've worked at U.S. Wal-Mart stores since December 26, 1998—as many as 1.6 million current and former employees. And whether Wal-Mart settles or pursues a courtroom battle, it could cost the retailer billions.

The women say that Wal-Mart pays female associates 5 to 15 percent less than males in comparable positions—even when the women have worked there longer and earned higher performance ratings—and that men are favored for promotions. The statistics certainly bear them out. At Wal-Mart, male assistant managers are paid, on average, $2,500 more annually than their female counterparts; male comanagers average $3,200 more; and male store managers, a whopping $16,400 more (that's more than a cashier—even a male cashier—earns in a *year*). Many other companies lack gender parity across employee ranks, but at Wal-Mart the clustering of women at the bottom and men at the top is stark: 92 percent of cashiers are women, and 85 percent of store managers are men.

Wal-Mart never posted openings for management training positions (at least, not until this suit was filed). Though standard operating procedure for most retailers, Wal-Mart considered this too inefficient and left it to individual store managers to promote from within the ranks. And, say the plaintiffs, "a strong corporate culture that includes gender stereotyping" ensured that more—far more—of those individuals were men.

One plaintiff said she was told she had to "doll up" to deserve a promotion. Others told of less-qualified male coworkers being granted transfers and assignments that had been denied them. One quoted her boss's reason for the preferential treatment of male employees: "God made Adam first."

Predictably, Wal-Mart appealed the court's class action certification, arguing that each employee's promotions and pay are determined by individual store managers, so only individual employees should be allowed to sue the company. The Ninth Circuit Court of Appeals agreed to hear Wal-Mart's appeal. As we went to press, no hearing date had been set, but it was expected to be in late winter or early spring 2005. Until that ruling is made, the case is on hold.

Haven't We Heard This One Before?

Bentonville has a couple of stock defenses that it trots out in response to each high-profile accusation of wrong-doing, from unpaid overtime to illegal foreign workers.

1. The "*I* didn't do it" defense (immortalized by Bart Simpson), with these variations:

   We knew nothing!
   That's not our policy.
   We are shocked, *shocked*.
   It was done by a few "rogue managers."

2. "We were working so hard for our customers, I guess we didn't pay enough attention to that *one tiny issue.*" Spokesperson Mona Williams, addressing the women employees' class action lawsuit, served it up thusly: "We've grown so quickly. We've spent so much time making sure we had a world-class distribution system and supplier network that we probably did not pay as much attention to making sure we got the personnel stuff right."

Awwww! Let's cut poor old Wal-Mart some slack, shall we?

Bentonville must issue the same scripts to all its spokespeople, because there's an uncanny echo among the corporate rejoinders.

CEO Leo Scott, on PBS's *Tavis Smiley* show: "So what we deal with today, on that issue [locking in after-hours workers], would really be the exception . . . a club manager who's a knucklehead and makes a wrong decision."

Mona Williams again: "When you have one million people working for you there are always going to be a couple of knuckleheads out there who do dumb things. But they are the exceptions. That's not Wal-Mart."

Oh, those darn *knuckleheads*! How did *they* ever sneak into the Wal-Mart ranks?

If This Story Doesn't Curl Your Toes, Nothing Will

Some Wal-Mart stories are so terrible that they make us sick to our stomachs.

Imagine a man under a restraining order going into a store—any store—and buying a shotgun without a single oral question being asked. . . . then going home and killing his twenty-two-year-old wife (mother of his two-year-old and five-year-old daughters), and his wife's brother.

And to make this all even more sickening, this happened in 1998, a year or so after the world's largest retailer of firearms supposedly stopped selling "Saturday night specials" over the counter.

(Remember: pistols can still be had from Wal-Mart via its catalog.)

The man who did all this is serving a life sentence in prison.

The family of the young mother of course sued, and Wal-Mart was ordered to pay the two little girls $16 million. It took nearly six years, but in February 2004 Wal-Mart finally agreed to settle for an undisclosed amount.

Meanwhile, qualifying members of the class are encouraged to join.

The plaintiffs will have to prove that Bentonville's top brass "exhibited malice or reckless disregard"—that is, that they were aware of the gender discrimination and did nothing to stop it.

This is one that Wal-Mart isn't going to be able to shrug

off, pay off, or drag out until everyone loses interest. It's a big-gie, and Wal-Mart's already scrambling to clean up its act in an uncharacteristically public way. At the annual sharehold-ers' meeting, officers described the steps the company's tak-ing to eliminate discrimination from pay and promotion prac-tices. Managers' bonuses will depend on their meeting workforce diversity goals, and management job openings will be posted rather than bestowed on the boss's favorites.

As one of the lead attorneys for the women puts it, "[W]ith a company the size of Wal-Mart, it's very hard to get their attention. . . . The impact of having a class action with 1.5 million women is that we get Wal-Mart's attention."

Sad to say, racism is still alive and well in this country. But racial discrimination and harassment are against the law, and when a worker has proof of such, the employer should make things right, especially if it's the biggest private employer in the nation and has taken a high-profile corporate stance that all who toil on its premises will be treated with fairness and re-spect. Wal-Mart discriminate on the basis of race? Heavens, no—that's not our policy! Wal-Mart turn a blind eye to racial harassment of its workers? Certainly not!

Ask Ben Guiliani of Augusta, Maine. As reported on sprawl-busters.com, he spent six years seeking justice from Wal-Mart in court. Guiliani, a man of Mexican descent, con-tracted with Wal-Mart to clean its parking lot in 1994. Wal-Mart employees on the night crew harassed and assaulted him; one said: "We don't like your kind." When Guiliani complained, the Wal-Mart manager told him he was overre-acting; the store ended his contract the following year. He filed a lawsuit, and four years later, at long last, a Bangor dis-trict court jury awarded him $650,000. Even after the judge later reduced this amount to $300,000, Wal-Mart appealed the case. The First U.S. Circuit Court of Appeals upheld the $300,000 award.

Did Wal-Mart pay up? Not a chance. The company hoped the U.S. Supreme Court would hear its argument, but in January 2000, the Supreme Court rejected Wal-Mart's appeal without comment.

Perhaps justice will come more quickly for twenty-two-year-old Daryal T. Nelson of Coldwater, Mississippi, who has the backing of the Equal Employment Opportunity Commission (EEOC) in his federal lawsuit. It charges that Wal-Mart discourages and unfairly rejects black applicants for truck-driver jobs at twelve distribution centers in the South—and that the retailer has hired some white drivers with worse driving records and less experience than the black applicants. Nelson is asking the courts to give his case class-action status; if granted, this could affect quite a few other job applicants.

When Nelson applied to Wal-Mart, he presented impressive credentials: good work history, truck-driving experience, a commercial driver's license, and a clean driving record. But Wal-Mart demanded one more thing from Nelson: a good credit rating. Nelson says this was not one of Wal-Mart's written requirements; he says it's selectively applied in favor of white applicants. He was offered a job, but when he reported for work, the area director denied him the driving job, based on "a gut feeling" that Nelson had presented a false credit rating and driving record. Instead, he said, Nelson could work at the center as a laborer.

Nelson filed a complaint with the EEOC, which found "reasonable cause" to believe he was the victim of discrimination and helped him file the lawsuit. Wal-Mart won't comment, except to say "We do not discriminate in our hiring practices."

We Get Letters . . .

A SCORCHED-EARTH POLICY

One of the things I've learned since the first printing of our anti–Wal-Mart book back in May of '98 is that Wal-Mart will seemingly go to any lengths to beat any lawsuit filed against it, however just the complaint.

Listen to this Kansas attorney:

> At some point in time, Wal-Mart will have to look at its self-insurance claims departments and wonder why 98 percent goes to defend claims and 2 percent goes to the injured (I am guessing at the percentages).
>
> In my recent dispute with Wal-Mart, I am sure $25,000 was spent by Wal-Mart to defeat a claim that could have been settled for under $10,000.
>
> Obviously, Wal-Mart has adopted a scorched-earth policy in the hope the injured will simply give up and go away.
>
> My client would have gotten nothing except for my determination to make Wal-Mart spend another $25,000 at a jury trial.

. . . And We Get Calls

We recently heard from a very successful supermarket owner in the Midwest. He had three thriving stores in his immediate area—these were sixteen-hour-a-day, seven-days-a-week operations with more than one hundred employees. Wal-Mart came to town and played dirty, very dirty. They sent one of their many assistant managers into our caller's store at odd hours and hired away his help at a dollar or two more per hour. At least one of them got burned: a less-than-loyal meat-market man he had trained took the Wal-Mart bait; shortly thereafter, Wal-Mart closed its meat market to stock only prewrapped meat.

6

FIVE WAYS WAL-MART IS A MENACE TO AMERICA— AND THE WORLD

In a grand sense, every fact and story in this book is about some way the mega-retailer puts the screws to an America that many of us still hold damn near sacred. When

- ✪ eyesore big-box stores loom on the outskirts of small towns and Main Street becomes a ghost town;

- ✪ folks who once strolled to do their errands, visiting neighbors along the way, must drive ten, twenty, or thirty miles on roads clogged with other "shopping commuters" or move;

- ✪ floods of cheap sweatshop goods from China and elsewhere force U.S. manufacturers to shut down factories here and set them up overseas, draining away hundreds of thousands of well-paying jobs;

you could say these are all ways the Wal-Mart corporation has hurt America.

Let's acknowledge, though, that this trend is not the exclusive province of Wal-Mart. There are plenty of nationwide chains to blame for the big-box stores, fast-food outlets, and strip malls that have replaced our communities' unique local colors with the same garish logos.

But Wal-Mart is different. Scarily different. Wal-Mart, with all its size, power, and influence, truly seems to believe it's above the law. In Bentonville, Arkansas, the grand plan has been laid out—and woe to anyone or anything that stands in the way.

In December 2003, *Fast Company* magazine stated: "[I]n its own category of general merchandise and groceries, Wal-Mart no longer has any real rivals. It does more business than Target, Sears, Kmart, J.C. Penney, Safeway, and Kroger combined." Wal-Mart continues spreading its dark shadow across the United States and is now well on its way in ten other countries.

In the company's 2004 annual report, CEO Lee Scott remarks cheerily, "At least once a day I am asked whether Wal-Mart can continue to grow. In the United States, Wal-Mart's sales are less than 10 percent of the retail market, and this year we plan to add more than 50 million square feet of new retail space. . . . a growth in square footage of more than 8 percent." What are they aiming for—100 percent? Oh, but that's just America. Beyond our borders, he notes, Wal-Mart's market share is even smaller. "So there is definitely room for growth."

You, dear readers, have had an earful from us already. Now, to sum up, here are the five most frightening ways in which the world's largest retailer is casting a pall over America—and the world.

MENACE #1: Stamping Out the Free Market

We don't claim to be experts about free-market economics—you know, capitalism, consumer choice, competing products and prices, "let the marketplace decide." But we can plainly see the country's biggest retailer becoming, in so many places, the only retailer in town (or several towns). We see that same retailer bent on phasing out competing manufacturers' brands and replacing them with its own private labels. In everything it does, Wal-Mart makes it plain that for them, the only acceptable competition is no competition. Wal-Mart's overwhelming power is placing our American free market in grave danger.

Whatever line of merchandise the Bentonvillains get into selling, they try to bully their way into becoming the number-one retailer of that industry's products. That's how Wal-Mart took over the retailing of bicycles and outdoor power equipment—the two industries for which Quinn Publications once produced trade journals directed solely to independent dealers. The Bentonville blankety-blanks became number one in bikes thanks in large part to many manufacturers bowing to their every demand. Now just try to find a Made-in-America bike.

Wal-Mart now rakes in 25 percent of all U.S. toy sales, thanks to a "toy price war" it launched in late 2003, just in time for the holiday sales season. The mega-retailer cut prices on a dozen of the "hottest" toys—making them all "opening price points." If your kid just had to have a Hokey Pokey Elmo, you could get it at Wal-Mart for 22 percent less than at Toys R Us. The *Wall Street Journal* noted that on average Wal-Mart's toy prices were 12 percent cheaper than Toys R Us prices, and 8 percent cheaper than Target's.

Then, surprise! The owner of high-end toy seller F.A.O. Schwarz, which had been struggling for a while, filed for bankruptcy. So did KB Toys. And in September 2004, the once-mighty Toys R Us admitted it was considering selling off its toy division.

KB's CEO Michael Glazer said the company had been

devastated by Wal-Mart's price war. "Except for a day or two here and there, it ruined our entire fourth-quarter business," Glazer said. "I know many malls have said they would like to keep us, just to have a toy store in the mix."

Indeed. That's also the wish of many customers who enjoy shopping at a mall with a full variety of specialty stores—something Wal-Mart is hell-bent on stamping out. Toy manufacturers are worried that the company's cut-throat pricing may force traditional toy stores, which carry a much more varied assortment than the discounters, to close.

The swath that Bentonville has mowed through the toy industry is just one example. Wal-Mart now sells more consumer electronics than anyone else—and dedicated sellers like Circuit City are feeling the pinch. As Wal-Mart muscles into the grocery business, twenty-five regional grocery chains have filed for bankruptcy.

The parent company of Toys R Us says it will separate its

floundering toy chain from its thriving Babies R Us chain. But it may be too late. Wal-Mart has begun creating its own dedicated departments for one-stop baby shopping.

MENACE #2: "The Law Is For Little People"

Pardon us for paraphrasing Leona Helmsley (you may recall the "Queen of Mean" hotel and real-estate magnate who sneered that "only little people pay taxes"). But the Benton-villains have proven time and time again that they really do consider themselves much too big to be bothered with pesky rules and regulations.

The sad truth of it is that all too often they get away with it. Whether mounting an aggressive defense against the most minor customer or employee lawsuit, or denying their guilt in environmental, trade, and labor violations, Wal-Mart's lawyers are ferocious fighters. They hate to settle. They appeal and appeal. They drag cases out for years.

Every so often—though not often enough—the retailer comes up against a large government agency, and loses. Oh, how sweet it is when we get word of one of those rare victories.

Since at least 1992, the U.S. Environmental Protection Agency (EPA) has been after Wal-Mart and its building contractors for violating terms of their storm-water permits under the Clean Water Act. If storm-water runoff—often carrying pesticides, chemicals, solvents, and other toxic waste—is not properly controlled at a construction site, it drains into waterways, killing fish and destroying habitat and possibly ending up in drinking water.

In 2001, the EPA cited Wal-Mart and several of its contractors for storm-water violations at seventeen locations in Texas, New Mexico, Oklahoma, and Massachusetts. It was the first federal enforcement action ever against a company for multistate violations of the Act's storm-water provisions. According to a Justice Department release, at one location the EPA found silt fences in disrepair and a visible trail of silt into an adjacent wetland. Wal-Mart and its contractor had also failed to regularly check that the storm-water controls were functioning.

The company agreed to a settlement that included payment of a $1 million civil penalty and a promise to establish a $4.5 million environmental management plan to improve compliance with environmental laws at all of its construction sites. Wal-Mart pledged it would make sure its contractors certified that all appropriate storm-water control measures were in place before construction began at new stores. It promised, too, to improve its oversight of environmental compliance at construction sites, monitor pollutant levels in storm water, and report these findings to the EPA.

But apparently Wal-Mart needed to learn its lesson twice. In the stepped-up EPA inspections that followed that settlement, fresh violations emerged at twenty-four sites in nine states—eleven of them in Colorado alone. The company had failed to get required permits, failed to institute a runoff-control plan, and failed to install controls to prevent discharges.

In May 2004, Wal-Mart agreed to a new settlement. It would pay the EPA a *$3.1 million* penalty. And it would pledge, once again, to meet a range of requirements. Wal-Mart must also spend $250,000 to help protect sensitive wetlands or waterways in one of the states. This could be in California, Delaware, Michigan, New Jersey, South Dakota, Tennessee, Texas, or Utah—but if there's any justice, it will be in Colorado.

And should the retailer get caught a third time, wouldn't it be grand if the EPA umpires could just tell Wal-Mart "three strikes and you're out"?

MENACE #3: Supercenter Consolidation

In the first edition, we sounded a warning about Wal-Mart's new Big Thing, the Supercenter: a megastore offering not only the whole range of goods that the old-style Wal-Mart might contain, but also such things as a supermarket, an auto service depot, a bank branch, a shoe repair shop, a video rental shop, a pharmacy, a restaurant (such as McDonald's)— just about every segment of a typical town's small business commerce that the original Wal-Marts hadn't previously driven out of business.

Even worse, when the retailer brings in a Supercenter, it often "consolidates"—systematically shutting down one, two, or three of the original Wal-Mart stores nearby, thus forcing all its customers to drive even farther to the "new, better, bigger, shinier" Wal-Mart Supercenter.

The overall expansion of the retailer's outlets continues, of course. At the start of year 2000 there were 721 U.S. Supercenters; as of December 2004, there were 1,672. Now that it has reached market saturation in many of the regions where it started, mainly the south and the Midwest, the retailer's sales growth at those stores is slowing. With much of its competition stamped out, Wal-Mart has "maxed out" its market share—of the goods and services that a typical Wal-Mart supplies, that is. Thus the steady branching-out into gas stations, car rental agencies, banks, and the other services provided by a small town's local businesses.

The way to kick up the amount of sales per square foot is to offer more goods and services in a single location, so that location (the Wal-Mart Supercenter) comes away with a larger share of the consumer's dollar, because the consumer has also done the grocery shopping, the banking, prescription drug and eyeglass purchases, car maintenance, and any number of other errands right there in the Supercenter.

This is all just cherry pie for Wal-Mart, but think about the way the landscape is starting to look for poor us in small-town America: Every fifty miles or so a great big shiny does-it-all Wal-Mart, and nothing, nothing, NOTHING in between. Where is competitive pricing going to be then, we wonder, when there are no competitors around? This extreme vision is our nightmare, but it's Wal-Mart's most cherished dream. Bank on it.

Shutting down stores and forcing customers to drive farther to a Supercenter (cheaper for Wal-Mart than running several stores) is one menace. Invading its last resistant American frontier—the cities—is another.

MENACE # 4: Laying Siege to the Cities

As we explained in our last edition, as Wal-Mart reached saturation in rural areas, it got interested in the urban outskirts and other resistant pockets of America. In the company's 1999 annual report, then-CEO David Glass remarked, "We think there may be some business that we are not getting purely because . . . [our stores] may not be as close to the customer or convenient for small shopping trips. That's where we think there may be an opportunity for the small grocery/drug store format. . . ."

Wal-Mart's solution for this was the "Neighborhood Market"—mainly a grocery store, with one-third devoted to general discount merchandise, plus a drive-through pharmacy. It sounded cozy, but it turned out to be an average of forty thousand square feet, covering about as much acreage as a football field. Hardly your mom-and-pop corner market.

As of December 2004, there were seventy-six Neighborhood Markets in the United States; the company planned to add twenty-five to thirty in 2005. However, Supercenters still seem to be the retailer's favored child: 240 to 250 new ones

The Small Grocery Store . . .Going . . . Going . . .Gone

One by one, the mom-and-pop grocery stores that were once the backbone of small-town America are disappearing. The Food Market Institute says their numbers dropped *40 percent* between 1988 and 1998. In 1993 Wal-Mart was not even in the top ten of grocery sales in the U.S.; by 2003, Wal-Mart sold the most groceries of any company in the United States.

In February 2000, Associated Press feature writer Josh Hoffner visited Dennis and Pam Hatzenbuhler of D & P Foods, the only grocery store in Flasher, North Dakota, serving this community of three hundred people for the last seventeen years.

"We're fighting tooth and nail to stay around," says Dennis. But with the likes of Wal-Mart choking out mom-and-pop stores, how long can they survive?

The problem now is getting suppliers who can justify "coming out this far"—to off-the-beaten-path retailers. And how can a small grocery compete with the Wal-Marts who buy by the trainload rather than the single carton?

Hatzenbuhler concludes, "The grocery business used to be a fun business, but now it's a stressful business. Customer loyalty is a thing of the past."

Maybe the Hatzenbuhlers can get a job at Wal-Mart . . . at near-poverty wages.

are planned, although only 80 will be entirely new "operating units," the rest replacements of closing stores or expansions of discount stores.

Wal-Mart has found the urban outskirts a tad tougher to penetrate than the rural areas and suburbs. In Wal-Mart's first attempts to set up shop within city limits in Chicago in 2004, the retailer went one for two.

Unlike the common rural or suburban scenario in which Wal-Mart demands millions in subsidies and tax rebates to locate there, the company has to shell out in the cities. For its siege of Chicago, it hired local legal experts and PR pros to counteract a well-organized opposition from the city's labor unions and promote itself as "a very good corporate citizen." Wal-Mart also took out a full-page ad trumpeting the benefits it would bring, and it reportedly paid telemarketers and pollsters to call up Chicagoans and coax them to demand a city council vote in Wal-Mart's favor.

Despite the stiff opposition from the unions and concerned citizens, the retailer managed to prevail in its bid to open a store in the predominantly black west side of the city. After a three-hour debate—with protesters in a roped-off area of the city hall's second floor chanting "One, two, three, four, we don't want your Superstore!"—the city council voted 32 to 15 to approve the store.

But Wal-Mart's investment in lawyers and PR flacks wasn't enough to win it another location it wanted on the south side. That vote it lost, 25 to 21.

Now normally a defeat like this would make Wal-Mart fight even harder. But at least some of the alders in Chicago knew all about the retailer's track record and what would likely happen if they let it into the Windy City. They countered the planned invasion with a proposed ordinance that would require big-box companies to pay a living wage, provide a minimum level of benefits to its workers, stay neutral if unions tried to organize workers, and promise not to use their mega-muscle to undercut and stamp out competition.

Alderman Joe Moore explained, "The philosophy is to make sure anyone seeking to do business in Chicago contributes to the overall economic well-being of the city.

The Wal-Marts Are Coming!
The Wal-Marts Are Coming!

We tried to warn them, but it was probably too late. . . .

On Thursday, June 17, 1999, two London newspapers contacted the author. Probable reason: Wal-Mart had bought the British retailer ASDA and would soon be arriving on their shores, bringing The Wal-Mart Way to merrie olde England. And this book of ours seemed to be the only one in the bookstores that's 101 percent pure anti–Wal-Mart.

First call: a thirty minute interview with a *London Telegraph* reporter whose questions pretty much centered around what Wal-Mart's competitors and vendors could expect when Wal-Mart begins operations in England. We painted the worst possible picture. The story, about eight hundred words, appeared in the following Sunday's *Telegraph*.

Next call: *London Sunday Mail* business editor Russ Hotten, asking if we'd be interested in writing a one-thousand-word story on Wal-Mart's forthcoming invasion. The *Mail* would pay $1 a word. (That's $280 more than we made in our very first year of newspapering.)

"Our" *Mail* story appeared the following Sunday (June 20, 1999). The headline was a grabber: **Ruthless retailer "has killed a way of life."** We laid it all out: the lost jobs, the squashed vendors, the scorched earth in Wal-Mart's wake.

Too late to stop the ASDA purchase. Perhaps not too late for our British cousins to arm themselves against the invasion from their former colony.

Wal-Mart Tries to Figure Out Germany

The way Wal-Mart blows its own horn on its growth, you'd think that their marketing genius is respected everywhere.

Not so in Germany, where the Bentonvillains have stubbed their toe in a big way. They started by buying two small store chains there in 1997, and as of this writing they've lost money every year. A big bundle!

When Wal-Mart goes into a country, they set a goal of 30 percent of the discount market. So far, they've captured only 5 percent in Germany.

Eight years along, they have a disappointing ninety-two stores there.

Why the big letdown? To begin with, Bentonville didn't quite get the German culture. Its "friendly, folksy" approach fell flat; for example, Germans were put off by greeters at the door. (Wal-Mart eventually caught on; now its German outlets are the only ones without greeters.) Second, Germany doesn't allow its merchants to sell goods below cost. That tied Wal-Mart's hands in slashing prices to dominate their competitors, whatever the cost. And Germany's a union-friendly place so they're not exactly thrilled

Without it, these businesses could end up costing the city economically with lost businesses and jobs at a faster rate than [businesses like] Wal-Mart provide. It's like the oil barons of a hundred years ago. The oil industry got so big and powerful that it resulted in no competition at all."

Wal-Mart then threw one of its classic hissy fits. With its contract for the South-Side store expiring, it pulled out, placing the blame on the threatened ordinance, which Wal-Mart Regional Director John Bisio claims "singles out just some—not all—businesses in Chicago." Then he darkly hinted that

with the U.S. retailer's anti-union stance. Finally, the German government limits retailers' operating hours so Wal-Mart's 24/7 operation was not allowed.

But in 2003 the German government expanded its closing-hour restriction from 6 to 8 PM. And wait'll you hear what Wal-Mart has done with those two hours. It's hosting "singles' nights"! That's right—now single German shoppers can find that special someone by pushing a shopping cart (with a discreet red bow attached to indicate romantic availability) through the aisles. It started on Fridays in Dortmund and has since spread to many other stores.

"Flirt points" are designated, with more wine and free chocolates. Lonely hearts can post their bios and photos on a bulletin board.

If you think Wal-Mart has abandoned its laser-like marketing focus to play matchmaker, think again. The retailer has trademarked the term "Singles Shopping." Special sales displays are stocked with romantic and singles-oriented merchandise. And those red bows on shopping carts? They're on *shopping carts*. No nervous single would want to just stroll around with an empty cart. To look relaxed and natural, you've got to fill it up.

Wal-Mart just might decide not to grace the West Side with the approved store there, either: "The reality is that, with these big-box ordinances looming, it could have an impact on whether or not we're able to go through with that project, as well."

When the going gets tough, the tough get to whining, don't they?

MENACE #5: International Expansion

Wal-Mart's drive for global domination, still in its early days when we warned you about it in our first edition, had taken

See Wal-Mart from the Temple of the Sun!

If you've ever been to Mexico City, you've probably heard of the ancient city of Teotihuacan, with its temple complex of pyramids, thirty miles north of the city. Perhaps you've even stood atop one of the pyramids, contemplating the long-lost civilization that built them and admiring the view.

The ruins draw hundreds of thousands of visitors each year. And now they can buy their souvenirs at Wal-Mart's new Bodega Aurrera discount store, which opened in November 2004 just a half mile from the two-thousand-year-old spiritual center.

The new store was opposed by the Front to Defend the Teotihuacan Valley—a coalition of local merchants, artists, actors, academics, and indigenous people's organizations that fought to keep the big box out and preserve both the cultural heritage and the livelihoods of many small shopkeepers. They carried banners reading "Don't Ruin Our Ruins," staged demonstrations and hunger strikes, and worked to raise international awareness of the threat.

All to no avail. The lure of "low prices" and one-stop shopping was just too strong. A lawyer for the opposition said they found more support from the international community than from residents.

One resident said the new store would save him time and money because right now he had to drive *ten minutes* to reach the nearest Wal-Mart. (Remember, Wal-Mart is now the biggest retailer in Mexico, with 623 stores and counting.)

Oh, dear. Hope he's prepared for Wal-Mart's inevitable consolidation in Mexico. That's when one or both of those stores will be left standing empty, and that resident and all the other customers will be driving for half an hour or more to reach the nearest Wal-Mart, because all the longtime local stores have been snuffed out. . . .

on real—and really terrifying—dimensions in our second edition. In Wal-Mart's 1999 and 2000 annual reports, special "International" sections charted the growth of the international division from its first profitable year in fiscal 1997. In 1998, then-CEO David Glass had estimated that in five years (by 2003), international sales might account for 10 percent of the company's total sales.

Now we've got a copy of Wal-Mart's fiscal 2004 annual report in hand, and it turns out that Mr. Glass *underestimated*. For fiscal year 2000, international sales made up more than 13 percent of Wal-Mart's $165 billion total sales. For fiscal year 2004, international sales made up *18.5 percent* of the $256 billion total. Wal-Mart is now the biggest retailer in Mexico and Canada.

In a May 2004 interview with the *Financial Times*, CEO Lee Scott wouldn't say just which countries in Europe the retailer planned to expand into (beyond the present Germany and the U.K.), but he "could not think of any country in Europe that we wouldn't want to be in over the long course of time." Scott called his trip to meet EU officials in Brussels a "charm offensive"—guess that was the European phase of Wal-Mart's ongoing campaign to remake its tarnished public image.

7

HERE'S WHAT YOU CAN DO ABOUT IT!

You've had an earful of the lowlife things Wal-Mart and the Walton family have pulled on you to make the Waltons about *100 billion dollars rich.* That's more than the GNP of the vast majority of third-world countries; more than the net worth of the entire Rockefeller family, heirs of Standard Oil, a company the U.S. government called a monopoly more than three-quarters of a century ago.

Wal-Mart is now the world's largest company. Deloitte Research says "They are so much bigger than any retailer has ever been that it's not possible to compare." In 2002, 82 percent of American households made at least one purchase at Wal-Mart. Of every retail dollar spent in the United States, Wal-Mart collects 7.5¢. It sells 32 percent of all disposable diapers, 30 percent of all hair-care products, 26 percent of all toothpaste. *Business Week* predicts that by 2010, Wal-Mart could be selling 50 percent of *all* such consumer staples.

What, you may say, can I as an individual possibly do to stop this company from taking over the world?

The statistics may be daunting—far worse than what we

reported in 2000. But the tide has turned against the mega-retailer. We said it in the introduction, you've seen the evidence all through this book, and even Wal-Mart knows it. Why else would it keep bleating about how it's so misunderstood and how all the mean things people are saying about it are so unfair?

In the battle to stop Wal-Mart from destroying America and the world, we have found the best weapon—*information*. We can combat Wal-Mart by *exposing the truth* and *spreading the word*. This book is our own humble effort to do just that.

We know this works. A prime example: employee turnover is so high at Wal-Mart because once folks actually get in there, they learn *the truth* behind all the smiley faces and bright blue vests and the promises about advancement opportunities. *Nearly half quit every year.*

This is a real problem for Wal-Mart. Their spokespeople can rave about the thousands of applicants they get every time they open a new store. But the CEO himself, in the 2004 annual report, laments, "In fact, our growth is not limited by access to capital. . . . Rather, our most significant challenge is attracting, retaining, and developing enough people who understand and embrace our culture and who can help us fulfill our growth potential."

Yes, it's hard to attract and keep workers when the truth about how Wal-Mart treats its workers is getting harder and harder to miss.

The truths in this book are just a starting point. (And believe us when we say there are *way* more true outrages, injustices, and horror stories about Wal-Mart than we could fit into these few pages.) *Your help is essential.* Whether you're a retailer competing head-to-head with the colossus, a supplier being squeezed to death by them, an "associate" struggling to get a fair deal, a citizen concerned about Wal-Mart coming to

Wal-Mart Damage Control

We do see an interesting shift in focus since we last took the plunge into a Wal-Mart annual report. In the 1999 and 2000 reports, Wal-Mart was cock of the walk: so confident, so full of itself and its glorious plans for conquering the world and covering it with smiley faces that—well, you really wanted to just smack 'em.

Not so in 2004. As we noted with cautious glee in our introduction, the world's biggest company is no longer America's sweetheart—and it knows it. So this year the message to stockholders is all about how wonderful, how selfless, how kind the mega-retailer is. Wal-Mart offers Good Jobs and Good Careers, gosh darn it! Wal-Mart doesn't pound mercilessly on its suppliers—it Builds Lasting Relationships with them. And Wal-Mart is Raising the Standard of Living for Its Customers. You can almost see the big guy blushing and shuffling its feet. "Aw, shucks, you don't have to thank us. It's just the right thing to do!"

But seriously, it looks like we foot soldiers in the anti–Wal-Mart ranks have had an effect with our websites, citizen groups, editorials, word of mouth, personal boycotts, local referendums. The word is out. Bentonville has noticed. They've had to change their message.

Don't stop now, folks. Keep that pressure on 'em!

town, or a consumer looking to your own bottom line and the well-being of your community, *you* can gain the satisfaction of a battle well waged in your dealings with Wal-Mart.

We'll start with five general approaches anyone could use, then detail a couple of dozen specific tactics for retailers, suppliers, citizens and planning boards, or consumers to try.

Can We Keep Wal-Mart Out of Our Cities?

Wal-Mart keeps nibbling away at the small, incorporated cities that surround the big urban centers.

But we doubt that the mega-retailer will rest until it gets its giant 200,000-plus-square-foot Supercenters into the big cities—not just one store per city, but several locations that will siphon off grocery business from the grocery chains (which, with all their faults, are better citizens by far than the Bentonvillains).

How to block the blankety-blanks?

First and foremost, it takes an attorney skilled in working with municipalities. As we understand it, a city's zoning and planning commissions can put up a lot of high hurdles for Wal-Mart to jump before they become the merchant of death to the independent businesspeople who are the backbone of your city.

If you live in or near Chicago, you know the battle that's under way there. You also know about this battle if you live in the Los Angeles area or the San Francisco Bay Area. Folks in other cities need to follow these stories and stay alert to those first signs of Wal-Mart nosing around their neck of the woods. Stay abreast of the news—and dig deeper than the local news stations do. Read the papers, check the Internet. Know the schedule and agendas for your city council and planning commission meetings.

Plenty of towns have fended off big-box stores, and you can learn from their successful strategies. A great starting point is the "Victories" page of www.sprawl-busters.com. It lists 248 winning towns, with links to articles about them and, for some, the addresses of websites they established for their successful campaigns.

Write Your Local Newspaper

The Letter to the Editor section of the local paper is every citizen's bully pulpit. Each issue gives you a free opportunity to speak out to a wide swath of readers. Your personal voice can be far more convincing than those full-page "letters" Wal-Mart pays to run. Study the letters to the editor that your paper prints to get a feel for the optimum length. Be sure of your facts, then speak from the heart.

Getting the truth out is most important *before* the Bentonvillains raise up a big box in your town. But if your town's already been Wal-Martized, you've still got plenty to say. Certainly, every merchant who's been put out of business should write a letter anytime and every time Wal-Mart does anything they don't like. For instance: for not supporting your local hospital's drive for money . . . or not pitching in and helping to pay for band uniforms . . . or football and basketball uniforms . . . or for a donation on a project your local Chamber of Commerce wants for your town. The possible grievances are as endless as Wal-Mart's greedy ways.

Write that letter!

Enlist Your Hometown Bank

You should also feel sorry for the home-owned bank (last we heard, there are still a few of these around) where you might be depositing your hard-earned money. They also got suckered when Wal-Mart came to your town. They might have believed that Wal-Mart would become a major depositor.

Not so. The bank's only gain is the measly fee it charges for taking the store's cash receipts via the drop-through night deposit box and wiring out the money the following morning to Wal-Mart headquarters in Bentonville, Arkansas—not leaving it long enough to "dust the floors," to borrow a phrase from *The New York Times*' depiction of how little independent banks benefit from a Walton Enterprises outlet.

And about those 100 new jobs Wal-Mart might bring to town? Well, for every 100 jobs Wal-Mart brings in, more than 150 jobs are lost in the area that particular Wal-Mart store serves. We should add that about 75 percent of those "new" Wal-Martians will be paid so little it's doubtful the bank would get more than a single handful of new depositors.

Bottom line: If and when you want to keep Wal-Mart from expanding its local (non-grocery) outlet into a Supercenter, try enlisting the president or chair of your bank to lead the drive. They should be well aware of the continuing threat to their industry.

Who You Gonna Call?

Sprawl-Busters! So far as we know, Al Norman is the number-one specialist in keeping a Wal-Mart from coming to your area—or keeping the Wal-Mart you have from expanding into a Supercenter.

Al is a former newspaperman who has dedicated himself to keeping Wal-Mart in particular—and big-box chains in general—from consuming Retailing America. His website, www.sprawl-busters.com, with its News Flashes from the front lines and Sprawl-Busting Victories, is a real shot in the arm for anyone who thinks that the fight's been lost. Don't you believe it!

Al's book, *Slam Dunking Wal-Mart!—How You Can Stop Superstore Sprawl in Your Hometown*, should be on every Wal-Mart hater's coffee table. We've read it. Liked it. Well worth the money. You can order it from his website (see above).

Norman estimates that one out of three stores Wal-Mart tries to build faces community opposition. Quite a few of these have called Al Norman for on-site consultation. You

Wal-Mart on the Web

Of course, the folks at Wal-Mart have become Web-savvy too. Seeing the fortune to be made in online selling, the Bentonvillains formed a joint venture with Accel Partners and launched their online store www.walmart.com in Fall 1999.

There's more to the site than shopping, though. With a little digging, you can unearth a rich trove of information. (Watch out, though, for the piles of horn-tooting hooey—they can really raise your blood pressure.) Start with "About Wal-Mart," "News Center," and "Investor Information" (annual report, proxy statement), then check out the menu of links on the left. You can stay abreast of the ever-growing outlet and employee totals and track specific new store openings, but we gotta warn you, these are not for the faint of heart. It's none too pleasant to contemplate the list of fifty-six towns getting new outlets in October 2004, or the fifty-nine being Wal-Martized in January 2005.

Be *sure* to explore the Supplier Information area, reached through the Company Information page, and look for a "Supplier Standards" document. The current

should too if you're even remotely expecting Wal-Mart to bully itself into your town or city.

Norman says that in the year 2004 "Sprawl-Busters and community groups . . . defeated more plans for big retail stores, most of them Wal-Marts, than in any prior year." In the first nine months of 2004 alone, at least sixteen cities and counties defeated plans for Supercenters—and twenty or more "pending" stores are being fought off by communities.

one's actually entitled *Factory Certification Report,* March 2003–February 2004, a disturbing view of overseas sweatshops where those cheap, cheap Wal-Mart goods are produced (for more, see chapter 5).

www.againstthewal.com This excellent portal site offers relevant media coverage from the past six months, with links to earlier six-month archives, as well as featured links to study reports and other Wal-Mart sites. Highly recommended.

www.walmartwatch.com Produced by the UFCW, this site is a real grab-bag of Wal-Mart news, stories, and facts.

Site upkeep seems a little ragged, and navigating through the links is sometimes iffy, but it's well worth poking around in. See too the union site itself, www.ufcw.org, which seems more actively maintained. Be sure to go to the Issues and Actions page and click the top link, "Wal-Mart Workers Campaign Info." Other UFCW-sponsored sites include http://www.union4walmart.com/websites.htm (a portal to many sites focused on regional efforts), www .walmartswaronworkers.com, and www.youareworthmore .org.

(continued)

Fight 'em in Cyberspace!

If you've got Internet access at work, at home, or at the library, you've got a direct line to an amazing wealth of information, from horror stories to organized opposition. Check out these anti–Wal-Mart websites (and Wal-Mart's own sites). (All URLs are current as we go to press; if you can't find them, try entering key words or phrases in your favorite search engine.)

Communities threatened by a new Wal-Mart are now set-

Wal-Mart on the Web (continued)

www.wal-martlitigation.com The home page of the Wal-Mart Litigation Project, which gathers, refines, and markets information about lawsuits against Wal-Mart. Co-ordinated by Nashville, Tennessee, attorney Lewis L. Laska, the project aims to "assist lawyers who sue Wal-Mart to force the company to act properly toward its customers and employees. . . . to 'level the playing field' so plaintiffs have a better chance of winning suits where Wal-Mart has done wrong." Unfortunately, on the site's "*Latest News—Newly Updated!*" page the news items are not dated, and many other pages seem unchanged since our last edition. Still, an interesting read, if only to reassure yourself that Wal-Mart is *not* above the law—or the lawsuit, anyway.

www.sprawl-busters.com This huge site, run by Al Norman, Greenfield, Massachusetts-based Sprawl-Busters consultant, "helps local community coalitions on-site to design and implement successful campaigns against megastores and other undesirable large-scale developments." Not exclusively focused on Wal-Mart; he takes on Home Depot, Kmart, and the like. But Wal-Mart stories dominate the "Breaking News Flash" section. It now has a terrific searchable news section.

ting up their own websites. For good examples, check the town links on the Sprawl-Busters "Victories" page, and visit the sites of

- ✪ The Southwest Springfield Neighbors Association (www.swsna.org);

- ✪ Stop Elitch Wal-Mart—an inspiring success story! (http://stopelitchwalmart.home.comcast.net/);

www.nlcnet.org Site of the National Labor Committee (NLC), whose mission is "to educate and actively engage the U.S. public on human and labor rights abuses by corporations." Full details about sweatshops (including Wal-Mart's deep involvement), NLC efforts to expose and reform them, and ways to get involved.

www.hel-mart.com This small, snappy site—with its logo of a malevolently grinning yellow smiley-face with devil horns—hawks irreverent anti–Wal-Mart T-shirts (guaranteed not made with sweatshop labor) and such. We have our eye on the shirt that reads "Hel-Mart: Always a Small Town Disaster. Always." They provide a good selection of anti–Wal-Mart links and a juicy collection of uncensored Visitor Feedback comments.

www.walmartclass.com/walmartclass94.pl Check this site for the latest on the class action lawsuit filed in April 2003 on behalf of over 1.5 million current and former female Wal-Mart employees (see chapter 5). In September 2004, the Ninth Circuit Court of Appeals agreed to hear Wal-Mart's appeal of the class-action designation, and a hearing was expected to take place in late winter or early spring 2005.

✪ Gig Harbor, Washington—With the snappy home-page headline "Us Against the Wal," the website of the Peninsula Neighborhood Association of Gig Harbor documents their (successful!) fight to keep out the big retailer (www.harbornet.com/pna/WalMart/walmart.html)

Got your armor on and your sword drawn? Here are twenty-three tactics for beating back the dragon.

Retailers

We've had scores of telephone calls and letters from independent merchants since the first edition came off the press in May '98, and we've gathered a baker's dozen of ideas you can use to fight back.

A Nixon fan we wuzn't, but let's give old Tricky Dick credit for saying, "When the going gets tough, the tough get going." Remember, you're fighting one of the most ruthless big companies in the history of American business—one of the toughest of the tough. So let's get going!

Try one, try them all—and give Wal-Mart hell.

1. MINIMIZE YOUR COMPETITIVE EDGE

That's right. Limit your exposure to Wal-Mart's competition by taking yourself out of competition as much as you can. One of the smartest merchants we know emphasizes that you can't—no way—compete with Wal-Mart by carrying the same brand-name merchandise. Simply visit your nearest Wal-Mart on a regular basis and make a mental note of the brands the discounter is stocking. Then stock a competing brand.

Another important component to this strategy is to *sell what Wal-Mart doesn't.* Tree Top Toys, a tiny seller in Washington, DC, makes a point of stocking products from smaller manufacturers that don't play with Bentonville. They don't stock Barbie, or this year's hot robotic character, or the well-known board games. No violent video games or warmongering action toys, either. But plenty of quality dolls, books, train sets—enduring favorites powered by kids' imaginations.

2. THROW YOUR WEIGHT AROUND

Eleven Argentinean vendors refused to sell to Wal-Mart, citing pressure from long-established retailers who carry the same lines Wal-Mart is discounting. (Wal-Mart's response, according to the *Wall Street Journal*, was typically charming: "[We] may have to import merchandise into Argentina and take business away from local workers.") This approach may not be viable for a number of small guys, but consider your vendor relationships in this light: they may be sick of dealing with Wal-Mart.

3. JUST SAY "NO"

The next time you go to an exposition, ask exhibitors whether they are selling to discounters. If the answer is "Yes," chances are you won't get a good discount. Bonus point: if you decide not to place an order, you may want to tell the exhibitor that this was a factor in your decision.

4. USE GUERRILLA TACTICS

Check out how one of South America's biggest discounters, Carrefour, is giving Wal-Mart Hell, with a capital H. According to the *Wall Street Journal*, "When Wal-Mart's new store prints a flier advertising bargains, the nearby Carrefour responds in just a few hours offering the same products for a few cents less—and the fliers are handed out at the entrance to the Wal-Mart parking lot." Hip! Hip! Hooray!

If you have the determination, the imagination, and the guts for a guerrilla campaign like this (even if it's a one-time deal, done on a smaller scale), you could poke a nice-sized stick in Wal-Mart's eye and have yourself some fun in the bargain.

5. FIGHT MARKETING AGREEMENTS THAT FREEZE YOU OUT

According to our local paper, the *Star-Telegram*, Fort Worth–area record store owner Bill Sowers launched a protest against the rock group Aerosmith in 1997. The group's label had made an exclusive deal with Wal-Mart to distribute its new EP. Feeling burned and righteous, Bill S. returned his entire stock of the group's other albums to the label. The cost to him will probably be about $1,000 to $2,000 in sales, all told, but God bless him!

For other store owners caught in a similar problem, here's a less gonzo approach: Enlist the help of your loyal customers. Publicize what's going on. Put out some fliers or a sign letting folks know of the cozy agreement between Wal-Mart and the record label—and telling them whom to write to if this ticks them off (give the label's address and email).

If customers in your store were actually looking for the new Aerosmith EP (or whatever), then they'll know why they can't find it, and they might be pretty upset—but not with you. (Some of them might just go over to Wal-Mart and buy the damn thing there, but you weren't going to get that sale anyway, were you?) Your sign makes it clear who's to blame, and the label might actually get some feedback from people they listen to: consumers. There's always a hope that, shown a downside, they'll be less ready to pull this crap the next time.

6. SELL MORE SHOES

A friend of a friend has a shoe store in a small Arkansas city of around twenty-five thousand. When Wal-Mart came to his town, he went right into their store, notebook in hand, to jot down every brand of shoes, socks, and stockings that would compete with his stock.

A week later, he had a sale on every brand that Wal-Mart was carrying.

Next, he called the shoe companies that he knew had refused to sell to Wal-Mart. From now on, he said, he'd also concentrate on odd sizes that he knew Wal-Mart wouldn't stock. He blanketed his sales area with newspaper ads that he could fit any foot.

He mailed a card to his regular customers: new lines of

shoes, more sizes, more up-to-date styles than they could find elsewhere.

Wal-Mart didn't faze this shoe specialist (oh, yes—he emphasizes specialist) even a wee bit. He's making more money now than ever before.

7. CURB SERVICE, IN THIS DAY AND AGE?

Curb service went out long ago, you say? Not down in our part of the country (Texas).

Just a few years ago we noticed the first Sonic Drive-In restaurant on University Drive here in Fort Worth. With waitresses on skates bringing trays right to your car, it took us back to the fifties (for those who remember, that was BWM— Before Wal-Mart).

Sonics were a little slow to catch on, what with a McDonald's every mile or so. But now, gosh, there are scads of Sonics in our area—even in a lot of small towns.

This doesn't just work for restaurants. Our old friend Milton Usry had a dry cleaning business. When you pulled up to drop off clothes, one of Milton's employees hit the curb to take 'em almost before you'd stopped the car.

Not only that—they knew which customers were coming to pick up an order, and by the time you reached the counter, they would have pulled it from the rack and had it waiting for you, ready to go. If you had to wait more than a minute, they'd cheerfully carry your order out to your car.

Milton, we should add, also did an excellent cleaning job, but that curb service was the little extra something that made him the number-one dry cleaner in town.

Oh yes. Milton retired a well-to-do man. A very well-to-do man.

That little extra something. Isn't that what we're all looking for?

8. IF SAM WALTON COULD DO IT, YOU CAN TOO

We wouldn't stoop so low as to read the late Sam Walton's autobiography. So we've gotten this secondhand: when Sam first started his chain of stores in small towns, he'd disguise himself in sunglasses and goodness knows what else, visit his competitors' stores, and make note of their prices—then go back to his Wal-Mart store and have his employees make new price tags for similar items, cutting the other stores' specials.

What's good for the goose is good for the gander. Here's what some of our readers have done.

One hometown guy told us he made weekly rounds to his local Wal-Mart and jotted down prices that were higher at Wal-Mart than at his store. He had "Compare Our Prices" fliers printed up: "Wal-Mart's price for _____ is $_____. Ours is $_____." He hired a boy to stand by an entrance road to Wal-Mart, handing fliers to every driver who'd take one. (If you do this, be sure your customers know about Wal-Mart's "opening price point" displays–those colossal towers of an item that's cheaper than cheap.)

Another mom-and-pop dealer was equally brazen. He did the same kind of price-checking, then painted comparison signs on his show windows for all passersby to see.

Remember, Wal-Mart does not always have the lowest prices on thousands of items. Let your customers know that Wal-Mart's are *perceived* lower prices.

9. HAVE YOU EVER SEEN A WAL-MART MECHANIC?

For half a century we owned trade magazines published exclusively for dealers who serviced what they sold—fifty years for our *Bicycle Business Journal*, thirty years for our *Outdoor Power Equipment* magazine. When dealers visited our booth at trade shows, we'd generally get around to asking them how they competed against Wal-Mart. These methods stand out:

- One bike dealer had a big sign in both his front window and shop asking, "Have You Ever Met a Wal-Mart Bike Mechanic?"

- An outdoor power equipment dealer had an equally eye-stopping sign: "Wal-Mart Lawnmowers Repaired Here."

- A bike/exercise equipment dealer in Indiana was disturbed when both a Wal-Mart and a factory outlet mall moved into his town. This prosperous two-store operator opened a third store adjacent to the factory outlet mall, and last we heard, his store in the heavy traffic area was the most successful of his three-store chain.

Remember: Wal-Mart mechanics are almost nonexistent. If you sell something that rolls or has a moving part, service is your number one selling point.

10. HOME DELIVERIES—WAVE OF THE FUTURE?

Picking up and delivering ain't one of Wal-Mart's specialties. So many things lend themselves to this extra touch that customers would appreciate in these busy-busy, no-time-to-do-it-all times.

Drugstores in competition with Wal-Mart should make home deliveries and advertise that they are able to provide that little something extra.

Clothing stores—both men's and women's—could deliver purchases that need alterations. Just like prescriptions, there's a good markup on apparel.

If that Domino man made hundreds of millions on delivering pizza, certainly all specialty restaurants should consider which of their foods could be delivered, hot and tasty, to the customer's door.

Yes, hundreds of Wal-Mart stores have rented space to local cleaners who expect you to drop off your clothes and pick them up. We've lost count of the cleaners in our town who probably would have stayed around if they had offered pick-up and drop-off services in our part of town on specific days of the week.

And think about pickup and/or delivery of items that need servicing (see tip #9). All those stores could increase business by offering such services.

Food for thought, anyhow.

11. HAVE A SPECIAL ON SOMETHING—ALWAYS

Way back when we were publishing the *Van Banner*, Van's main grocery store was owned by a grouchy old man who made up in salesmanship for what he lacked in personal warmth. His store was a small, run-of-the-mill type, and all his prices were pretty much the same as the other four grocers, with one exception. In the middle of his store, he always had a HUGE STACK of some kind of canned goods—beans, corn, hominy, whatever his wholesaler had on special—that he could sell for a penny or two less per can than his four competitors in town. An eye-catching sign near the entrance trumpeted "Three cans for 49¢, four cans for 69¢." That's all it took for the shoppers of Van to perceive that his were the cheapest prices in town.

12. IF YOU DON'T HAVE A COFFEE ROOM, GET ONE

We've seen this happen so many times that we know it works.

For some twenty years we bought all our cars from the same dealer. Seems you can't avoid twenty or thirty minutes of "haggling" time: color, leather or plush seats, winterizing, price, terms of payment. . . . Our old salesman, Al Hewitt, always took us to the company's coffee room to "talk it over." Free coffee, of course, or a soda from one of the dispensers if Al felt like springing for that much.

This coffee room bit is intended, of course, for dealers of higher-ticket items.

Higher price tags were certainly the order of the day when we went to wife Lennie's favorite dress shop here in Fort Worth, Mary McCauley's. Mary's husband, Jim, has a particular knack for making husbands feel at ease. He always met us with, "I've got coffee, decaf, tea, white and red wine, and Cokes. What'll you have?" Said in such an inviting tone that if you didn't take one or the other, you'd be insulting him. So we took. And Lennie bought. And bought. And bought.

We've been in hundreds of bike stores in our fifty years of publishing dealer trade journals; several of the more successful places offered comparable hospitality. Particularly appreciated when you remember that the better bikes sell from $600 and up.

Remember that Wal-Mart has never been known to give anybody anything for the sake of hospitality and good will.

Take advantage of that. Somewhere in your store there's room for it. If nothing else, curtain off a place in the back—and serve those loyal customers from a fresh-brewed pot.

13. SELL AMERICAN; BUY AMERICAN

One of the biggest advantages independent retailers have over Wal-Mart is that the Bentonville Bullies can almost be classified as anti-American in their buying of men's and women's apparel and shoes.

Every—repeat, every—independent dealer should look for the label on every item that could be classified as fast-moving merchandise, and run "Made in America" ads in your local newspaper on a regular basis. By all means, make that headline as big as you can—**MADE IN AMERICA**—on brands not sold by Wal-Mart. And how about a small fight-back line like "CANNOT BE FOUND IN WAL-MART STORES"?

Believe it: the more you play up "Made in America," the sooner American factories can regain some of the jobs they've lost to slave labor in overseas plants.

Suppliers

If you sell to Wal-Mart and they are killing you on the margin, there's just one thing we can recommend that you consider:

14. DON'T PLAY

According to the *Wall Street Journal*, the toy manufacturer Step2 decided not to supply to Wal-Mart, joining a number of manufacturers who refuse to deal with Wal-Mart and other mega-retailers with "mighty retail clout." Apparently the manufacturers simply can't stomach the huge discounts at which the retailers sell their products (not to mention the other squirrelly things Wal-Mart does to its vendors—see chapter 3).

In the wake of the Bentonvillains' brutal price war on competing toy sellers, some toy makers banded together and agreed to draw the line. They'll offer exclusive launches of new products to Wal-Mart's competitors; for example, Toys R Us alone got to carry Wild Planet Toys' interactive Aquapets for three months before its general release to the mass merchandisers.

Citizens and Planning Boards

If Wal-Mart or another big discounter is sniffing around your town, look out! Now's the time, when you still have power, to make preparations.

15. OVERHAUL YOUR TOWN'S COMPREHENSIVE PLAN

Check out the steps outlined by the Lancaster County Planning Commission in chapter 2 (pages 29, 31). These four steps, taken with foresight and thoughtfulness, will go far toward "Wal-Mart-proofing" your town. Warning: these steps take time and are best for those towns that don't have a fight looming on the horizon.

16. MAKE ZONING APPROVAL PROCESSES MORE STRICT

This is a corollary to 15, above. Wal-Marts are invariably built away from downtown, often in an as-yet-undeveloped area. This means that, in order for a Wal-Mart to be built, the developer who owns the building will have to get zoning changes so they can meet requirements for sewer, drainage, and traffic accommodation.

Now, some forward-looking local merchants with political clout are asking city councils to rewrite the city's bylaws to demand that any request for zoning changes must be approved by at least a two-thirds vote of the city council. This would certainly tend to make a quiet and sneaky incursion by Wal-Mart much more difficult.

Some smart towns and cities are now crafting specific ordinances designed to curb the easy entry of big-box retailers. Chicago, for example, may soon require big-box companies to pay a living wage, provide a minimum level of employee benefits, not oppose union organizing, and compete fairly with local businesses. A little Internet research should produce some ordinances your municipality could adapt.

17. HOW ABOUT A GOOD OLD-FASHIONED PETITION DRIVE?

This tried-and-true (and relatively easy) form of protest was part of the drive to keep Wal-Mart out of Westford, Massachusetts. Many of the five hundred folks who signed the petition went a step further, wearing "If they build it, we won't come" buttons in the weeks before the petition passed. Find out your town's petition protocols, get some clipboards and pens, and enlist your friends and neighbors.

18. ENLIST HOSTS OF CALL-IN RADIO SHOWS

Does your town—or one nearby—have any call-in radio shows? They're always looking for a subject that will attract listeners. There are few souls out there in radioland who are neutral about Wal-Mart. Just think of the really juicy things you could raise hell about on a call-in show. Here's a few to get you started:

❂ Wal-Mart's near-total lack of support for local institutions (hospitals, churches, charities, etc.).

❂ Wal-Mart's notoriously frequent calls to police about shoplifters and other disturbances. Shouldn't Wal-Mart be made to pay for excessive police calls, just as you might

"We Don't Want Your Lousy Store!"

Think your town's too small to mount a defense against the retail giant? If Tijeras, New Mexico (pop. 310), can stop 'em, so can you. In July 1997, Tijeras got wind of plans for a 155,000-square-foot Supercenter, even though Wal-Mart already had a handful of stores within twenty miles, not to mention several outlets in nearby Albuquerque.

A coalition organized to stop the project: the East Mountain Citizens Against Wal-Mart, the East Mountain Neighborhood Defense Fund, the East Mountain Legal Defense Fund, and the Bernalillo County government. At a town hall meeting, Wal-Mart opponents stood outside chanting "One, two, three, four, we don't want your lousy store!"

Finally, the mayor of Albuquerque swore he'd block any water or sewage lines to the Supercenter. In June 1999, Wal-Mart withdrew, having spent $300,000 on property-development studies and consultants. And as of 2005, Tijeras has kept 'em out.

Yes, Wal-Mart can be turned back if a town or city's officials get their dander up and are willing to invest a few thousand dollars in attorneys' fees to make it all legal.

be charged for service calls when you keep triggering your own burglar alarm?

✪ Shouldn't some of Wal-Mart's employees (said to be about 40 percent of the Wal-Mart workforce) be eligible for at least some of the benefits other employees are getting?

✪ All the trashy, smelly garbage that Supercenter grocery departments and in-store eateries generate: how do the folks living near a Wal-Mart feel about that—and all the noise that comes from those parking lots?

❂ And what about those guns Wal-Mart sells; should it be allowed to operate that department in your hometown?

19. KNOW WHOM YOU'RE VOTING FOR

In its latest annual report, Wal-Mart announces these expansion plans for fiscal year 2005: 25 to 30 new Neighborhood Markets, 40 to 45 new discount stores, and 80 or 90 brand-new Supercenters—plus relocations or expansions of 160 existing discount stores into Supercenters. Mind you, this is just in the United States; 155 to 165 new units are planned for the rest of the world. And in 2006 . . . who knows?

So now, more than ever, it's important to know whom you're voting for in your next city election. Ask—demand—that the candidates for city council tell you, and the public, how they feel about Wal-Mart's plans to monopolize your town.

20. RUN FOR OFFICE

Jerry Greenfield, of Ben & Jerry's Ice Cream fame, did just this in his town of Williston, Vermont. He ran for city office for the express purpose of voting against a mall that would have Wal-Mart as one of its tenants. If you care enough about your town to take a major stake in the future of its development, a local office might just be the place for you to do some good work. It is surprisingly easy to run for office on the local level, and it's something to think about if you are ready to take the next step in civic commitment.

21. USE YOUR FIFTEEN MINUTES OF FAME

Artist Andy Warhol once said, "In the future everyone will be famous for fifteen minutes." Once you get involved in your local campaign to stop the Wal-Mart invasion, you just may find yourself on the local news . . . or even on the network. Be prepared. Think about what you'd say is wrong with Wal-Mart, why your town doesn't want it, and what ordinary folks like you can do to stop it. Don't be shy. Make the most of it!

I've had my fifteen minutes—er, seconds. It was mid-1999, just about the time Wal-Mart "invaded" Great Britain. We got an early call from the New York office of ABC news anchor Peter Jennings, asking if we'd be available for that evening's broadcast. Would we? Damn right we would! . . .

Within minutes, the ABC Dallas office dispatched a camera crew to my hometown of Grand Saline, Texas, to scan the deserted store buildings emptied in the wake of two nearby Wal-Mart Supermarts, and I had an appointment at the local ABC office for a camera interview.

My time on that night's Wal-Mart segment ran less than a minute—way less. More like fifteen seconds. Whoever edited that segment owes me about fourteen minutes and forty-five seconds of fame. But, what the hell. My old wrinkled face, my name, and the title of my book did appear on some six million TV screens on Wednesday, June 30, 1999. A glimpse of celebrity we'll pass on to my granddaughter's children.

Consumers

22. COMPARISON SHOP

I'd tell you to check prices and write them down for comparison with another retailer's, but Virginia Berger of Spring Hill, Florida, tried to do just that and was told by the Wal-Mart staff that jotting down their prices was "against store policy." Whew! Now why could that be? Could it be because study after study has shown that Wal-Mart's prices are, for the most part, not lower than discount competitors—that they are, in many cases, substantially higher?

A Conscientious Choice

If you're hooked on Sam's Club, consider shopping at some other gigantic warehouse outlet that treats its workers far more decently. We can't tell you where to shop, of course, but we can mention that Costco puts its employees second (after its customers), *ahead of its shareholders*.

Wall Street finds this outrageous. Grumbled one retailing analyst: "Costco's benefits are overly generous. Public companies need to care for shareholders first." But Costco CEO James D. Sinegal says, "We think when you take care of your customers and your employees, your shareholders are going to be rewarded in the long run. And I'm one of them [the shareholders]; I care about the stock price. But we're not going to do something for the sake of one quarter that's going to destroy the fabric of our company and what we stand for."

Costco offers the best wages and benefits in retail,

If you want to determine which store or stores in your area actually have the lowest prices overall, why not check it out (even if you have to use your excellent memory or a mini tape recorder)? Some of you have the luxury of not having to bargain-hunt on everything you buy, from toilet paper to mac-and-cheese, but it would be nice to know who you can trust, in general, to be giving you a good price. And it may not be the much-hyped discounter.

Of course, it is this kind of conscious buying that Wal-Mart wants you to escape entirely: Everything all in one place! One-stop shopping! If not the lowest price, at least one that looks fairly competitive! Just remember what kinds of things you are giving away when you give away your power as a con-

paying employees an average of $15.97 an hour. Its health-care coverage is vastly better than Wal-Mart's: 82 percent of Costco employees are covered, the enrollment waiting period is much shorter (six months for part-timers, versus two years for Wal-Mart's part-timers), and Costco workers pay only 8 percent of their health-care premiums, compared with Wal-Mart associates' 34 percent.

Strangely enough, Costco's annual employee turnover is 17 percent, compared with Wal-Mart's 46 percent.

Costco follows another practice that impresses us mightily: the CEO caps his pay at twice the salary of a Costco store manager.

But you're deciding whether to be a customer. Well, among all the other good reasons, consider that Costco has a "no receipt, no questions asked, no time limit" return policy (except for computers, and even for those you get a generous six months). Just try getting that kind of service at Wal-Mart.

sumer to the big discounters, and consider what they are reaping in return: massive profits and huge growth, the blind arrogance of a mighty corporation, and the ruin of the texture of so much of small-town America's commerce and society.

23. CHOOSE WHICH KIND OF COMPANY YOU SUPPORT

Low price shouldn't be the only factor in your purchase decisions. If you've got the wherewithal to spend more than the lowest price, consider the ethics and practices of the stores you patronize. How do they treat customers? How do they treat employees? And will the dollars you spend there recirculate locally or be sucked away to some other state?

We Get Letters . . .

THIS COULD TURN INTO A MOVEMENT.

Here's the perfect letter to round out this chapter and bring our book to a close. What's the simplest, easiest thing you can do to stop Wal-Mart? Just say "No" to shopping there and talk your family and friends into doing likewise. Dana Buse of Tupelo, Mississippi, expresses that spirit beautifully. We think your boycott is just dandy, Dana, and we thank you for spreading the word.

> I have just read your book. . . . and wanted to write and tell you that I appreciate your efforts in letting consumers know just what type of company they are dealing with if they choose to spend their hard-earned money with Wal-Mart. A few years ago I launched my own little boycott against the behemoth retailer and I feel even more justified in doing so now. [I started] because the little Wal-Mart discount store closed [when] a second Supercenter opened in my town. There was no more "just running in" to pick up a few items. It became a chore: The parking lot was so huge that I always ended up parking about a mile from the entrance, what few items I needed were always on opposite sides of the store, and I could never remember what side certain items were on (the grocery side or the "regular" side); out of about fifty registers, only five would be open. I could go on, but you probably get the idea. Unless I was out of EVERYTHING in my house, it just became too much of a hassle. So I decided to just see how long I could go without having to darken the doors of the Supercenter, and lo and behold, it's been about four years now. At first, it was just a little contest I had going on just for myself, but now it is a full-fledged boycott,

now that I've learned quite a bit about the tactics they employ.

No one I know can believe that I could live without Wal-Mart. I try to tell them it isn't impossible—it just took some getting used to. If everybody would put their minds to it, I believe Wal-Mart could be brought down SEVERAL pegs. It would take time, yes, but it could be done. But with this fast-paced society, most people like not having to go from store to store to get their shopping or errands done. I don't have any children, but I can imagine the temptation to just try to get in as much from one store as possible without having to drag the kids from store to store after working all day—or not wanting to spend my whole day off doing so.

It is so amazing to me that my "gut" instincts always seem to know. . . . since my boycott, I've just had the feeling that Wal-Mart isn't the great, wonderful company it tries to portray itself as. Just a few weeks ago, *A&E* ran the biography of Sam Walton and I remember thinking *What a greedy, ruthless !*?!*!*. Before, I had the impression that he was just a savvy, hard-working, smart old man who really was a caring person. HA! That's not what I saw. It's like [for him] no other retailer or small town merchant has THE RIGHT to make a living. What is presented as good old American competition is really a quest for world domination. . . .

Soon it won't be enough to be the only retailer in town; they'll purchase and acquire companies that aren't their real competition. Wal-Mart is so huge and far-reaching and ruthless, when will they have enough? It makes me think of the anti-Christ. Scary!!!

My goal is to try to convince every person I know to stop spending their money at Wal-Mart or at least try to spread some of it around with other retailers. I know this will be a lengthy, uphill battle, but if everyone did this, after a while it might start to affect Wal-Mart. What I would LOVE to see happen to Wal-Mart is what happened to Enron and WorldCom and other mighty corporations who have fallen beyond repair. Not through fictitious accounting, but from consumers turning their backs on them. That is not nice to wish on anyone, let alone a company that has employees that depend on them, but they need to have a dose of what they've done to others . . . Have you ever noticed how some people in the world just bully, lie, steal, cheat, and act as if the rules don't apply to them through life? And someone will say, "Oh, they'll reap what they sow" or "He'll get his one day," yet they never do. People just accept this and don't seem too offended. If I tried that, I wouldn't get away with it, let alone become a billionaire . . . This is how I see Wal-Mart. Classic parable of the schoolyard bully that everybody just tries to stay out of his way and just hope and pray they don't get squashed and are too chicken to try to stand up to. Well, maybe I won't be able to single-handedly change them or drive them out of business, but I sure am not going to give them my money either. They won't be able to count me as one of the millions who've made them billions.

Thank you for letting me vent. I know I don't have a personal Wal-Mart nightmare to share with you, but I thought you would want to know that some people don't need a reason to despise them. The very existence of Wal-Mart is more than enough reason.

God bless you and thanks for your efforts. They DO make a difference.

The long and the short of it for us is, we hate Wal-Mart. We'll never set foot in another of those emporiums as long as we live, and we'll fight them to the bitter end.

You, on the other hand, may choose to shop at Wal-Mart; you may even be happy to have a Wal-Mart in your town. There are legitimate reasons to shop there and real reasons why people welcome Wal-Mart into town.

All we ask is that if you do decide in favor of Wal-Mart— whether you're shopping for a barbecue grill there or permitting the mega-retailer to build in your town—just know what you are choosing, and know what you are choosing to give up and what you may be allowing to be destroyed.

Readers

In the first two editions, we invited you to chime in, and did you ever! Your calls and letters have confirmed our worst suspicions about the Bentonville blankety-blanks—and given us hope that we shall yet rise up and smite them! We've shared with you in these pages some of our favorite responses (see the "We Get Letters" and "And We Get Calls" sections at the end of most of the chapters).

We'd still love to hear from you about your encounters with Wal-Mart. Please write to us if you'd like. Send your letter to Bill Quinn, c/o Ten Speed Press, P.O. Box 7123, Berkeley, CA 94707.

Former Wal-Mart Employees

Keep letting us know why you told Wal-Mart to take the job you had and shove it. Send your letter to Bill Quinn, c/o Ten Speed Press, P.O. Box 7123, Berkeley, CA 94707.

Independent Merchants

Merchants who have been put out of business; storekeepers suffering from Wal-Mart's business tactics—tell us your stories! Writing on your letterhead would be great, but you can also use scrap paper and send it to Bill Quinn, c/o Ten Speed Press, P.O. Box 7123, Berkeley, CA, 94707.

Vendors/Suppliers

We know how you've suffered financially as a result of Walton Enterprises. Write to us about your mistreatment. We guarantee that your letter will be kept 101 percent confidential, unless you tell us that it's okay to publish. Send it to Bill Quinn, c/o Ten Speed Press, P.O. Box 7123, Berkeley, CA 94707.